THEOLOGY AND THE CAIN COMPLEX

Richard Hughes
Lycoming College

UNIVERSITY
PRESS OF
AMERICA

Copyright © 1982 by

University Press of America, Inc.

P.O. Box 19101, Washington, D.C. 20036

Printed in the United States of America

ISBN (Perfect): 0-8191-2358-7
ISBN   (Cloth): 0-8191-2357-9

Library of Congress Catalog Card Number: 81-43698

For my

Father and Mother

William and Dorothy Hughes

Acknowledgment

Unless otherwise stated the biblical quotations are taken from the Revised Standard Version of the Bible, copyrighted 1946, 1952, © 1971, 1973 by the National Council of the Churches of Christ in the U. S. A., Division of Education and Ministry.

Table of Contents

Preface

This book was begun in the summer of 1978 and completed exactly two years later. The major psychiatric portions were read and criticized by Dr. Leopold Szondi of Zürich, Switzerland. The biblical discussions were critically evaluated by my senior colleague Dr. Eduardo Guerra of Lycoming College. My belief in the complementarity of science and religion has grown out of discussions with my former teacher Dr. Harold Oliver of Boston University. The contributions of these scholars to my thesis are deeply appreciated. But the responsibility for any errors or limitations in this book is mine alone.

The general development of my work has also been facilitated by conversations and correspondance with the following: Dr. Harry Slochower, President of the Association for Applied Psychoanalysis; Dr. Karl Bürgi-Meyer, Director of the Szondi Institute in Zürich; Dr. Dietrich Blumer of the University of Michigan Medical School; Dr. Vera Roboz of Camberwell, Australia; Professor Claude van Reeth of the University of Paris; Dr. Werner Huth and Dr. Dankwart Mattke of Munich, West Germany; Rev. Dr. Maurice Bairy and Rev. Hugo Enomiya-Lassalle of Sophia University in Tokyo, Japan.

The manuscript was prepared for publication by Esther Henninger. Her cordial diligence and competence are sincerely appreciated. My wife, Diane Hughes, helped me in typing the several drafts of the manuscript. She was also an active participant in the research, conversations, and travels that shaped the material of this book.

Williamsport,
Pennsylvania

Introduction: A CONCEPT OF DESTINY

I. The Theoretical Framework

The aim of this book is to present a theory of human destiny as it is informed by the contemporary experience of evil. While ethical issues are in the forefront, the following chapters will stand within the general area of Christian theology. In current discussions theology is a fluid, diverse, and unsettled field. Whether Protestant, Orthodox, or Catholic, we can easily discern a wide variety of schools. Some of these are the process, hope, and liberation theologies, investigations into the meaning of myth and symbol, and research concerning the nature of life and death.

When considering the field as a whole, it seems that the dominant current issue is the meaning of the life span. A process theologian, a student of death and dying, and an interpreter of stories all share the belief that life has a purpose, a direction. This parallels the modern research of sociologists and biologists into patterns of behavior. Recently, advances in microbiology and medical genetics have opened up even more insights into the determinants of the life span. The length of life is generally fixed at birth. The life span of the individual is directly proportionate to the duration of the cells in his or her body.[1] For when we take cells out of our tissues, put them into a nutrient culture, they will divide so many times and then stop.

We who have cared for dying individuals in hospitals can confirm that, as the end of life draws near, the patient may confess something like this: "life has a pattern."[2] Similarly, in dramatic near-death encounters, when we suffer reversible comas, heart attacks, or serious injuries, we may, in a few seconds, behold the so-called "life review."[3] Suddenly, in the face of mortal danger, our whole life is recalled before our mind's eye, as though it were a final summary, a last judgment. Whether disclosed by a near-fatal accident, or confirmed in a laboratory, it appears that the human life span is a specific allotment.

All of these investigations, both religious and scientific, tacitly presuppose a common but unexplained theme--human destiny. It is a sense of destiny that a theologian assumes when he or she encourages us to put our lives into story form. It is the same vision of destiny in the mind of the dying cancer patient who knows that life has come to a climax. The sense of destiny seems to be the fundamental issue that cuts across all boundaries and reveals new insights into human experience. But so far as I know, no American theorist has attempted to formulate explicitly a theory of destiny.

In order to fill in this gap, I will draw upon the work of a distinguished European psychiatrist who has made the problem of destiny central. Appealing to a medical colleague should not be surprising; for American theologians have long been interested in the research of such physicians as Sigmund Freud, Carl Jung, Victor Frankl, and others. But there remains the work of a man whose labor has not yet been fully appreciated. He has been described as the most original and learned genius since Freud.(4) His name is Szondi.

Leopold Szondi has formulated a new way of looking at things. He has produced, mainly in German, an immense body of literature which bears the name Schicksal psychology or destiny analysis. Despite the massive and technical character of his works, there are a few seminal ideas that may help us in the field of theology. Szondi's theory of destiny is neither deterministic nor occultic. It is quite precise and practical.

The simplest way to comprehend our destiny is to take a look at our families as they extend over several generations. When we go back over the lives of our parents, grandparents, aunts, and uncles, we can see various patterns. We may discover, for example, that a grandmother and grandfather eloped, only to be followed by their own daughter who married the same way. We will surely find repetitions in sickness and the choice of vocations. We may even be shocked to discover that you and I are acting in the same ways as our ancestors.

The pivotal concept in the new psychology of destiny is the familial unconscious. Most theological students are acquainted with Freud's personal and Jung's collective unconscious. The familial is that mysterious intermediate region generally overlooked by individualistic and environmentalist pursuits. Yet the silent, largely unexplored dimension of the ancestral memory contains the sources of our destinies. After decades of medical and biological research, Szondi has decoded the workings of this dimension.

It is well known that each of us inherits half our genes from the father and half from the mother. In the formation of the zygote the genes are grouped in pairs within the chromosomes. If I receive from both my parents genes for blue eyes, then I will get blue eyes. But if I acquire a gene for brown eyes from my father, and one for blue eyes from my mother, then I will probably have brown eyes. The difference is that the brown eye gene is usually dominant, the blue eye gene recessive. A dominant gene has the strength to come out in the physical appearance of the offspring. A recessive gene must be paired with its correlate before the respective tendency can become dominant.

Although the research is still in progress, we know that heredity is not for strictly physical characteristics. We can also inherit potentialities for illness and constitutional dispositions. The current medical estimate is that each of us carries four to eight lethal genes.(5) These include the susceptibility to a wide range of disorders. The reason why we may not actually contract some of these diseases is that we inherit them recessively. In the reshuffling of the genetic information at the moment of conception a normal and an abnormal gene are paired for a specific tendency. With such a mixture we become heterozygous for that tendency.

Even though a recessive tendency remains latent, and is not manifest, it retains its form. It may be transmitted for several generations until, at an opportune conception, it is mixed with its identical corollary and becomes manifest. This dimension of latent, recessive genes is what American scientists have called the genetic load. In Szondian psychology it is the familial unconscious. Whatever it is called, the recessivity which we receive at the time of our conceptions can be influential in our destinies.

This can be illustrated quite simply. Of the four to eight lethal genes that most families transmit, tendencies toward the major psychiatric disorders are present. These include schizophrenia, epilepsy, and manic-depression. For example, schizophrenia is inherited recessively. So to be susceptible to this disease, I must receive the gene from both parents. If I receive a mixture of a normal and an abnormal gene, I will not be schizophrenic. But I may show schizoid tendencies such as aloofness, narcissism, preoccupation with abstract ideas and fantasies. When faced with a crisis, my inclination is to fall back upon these characteristics as a defense.

The study of a family tree is important in detecting such patterns. Wherever a lethal tendency appears in the family line, such as epilepsy or manic-depression, it remains as a possibility, capable of coming out in any descendant. This is particularly true when we are confronted with crises. In times of conflict, when our lives appear to be in turmoil, a latent tendency can surface as a symptom of the unresolved predicament. This is how diabetes, allergies, ulcers, and migraines often have their onset. These particular ailments are genetically related in the broad epileptoid group.

The key to detecting the familial unconscious is the crisis-oriented personal decision. We may put choice on a continuum along side the symptom, which expresses the personal unconscious, and the symbol or archetype, from the collective. While symptoms and symbols accompany our destinies, the decisions unfold them. The choice makes the destiny. However, it is not the ordinary or trivial choice. The crucial destiny-making decisions are primarily those of marriage, vocation, and personal friendship. In a less personalistic sense, but equally precise, sickness and mode of death are also such choices, in so far as they are goal-directed activities that come out of the depths of the organism. It is true for such fatal illnesses as cancer and heart disease. These run in families and are at present of epidemic proportions.

For some people decision-making is free, creative, and ennobling. They are permitted to speak of a destiny in a lofty sense. But for most of us, our decisions are not so easy; they are difficult, compulsive, and often filled with anxiety. To the extent that finding a mate or getting a job are rarely rational enterprises, these choices may not escape an unconscious familial influence. When such decisions are crippling and destructive, we may then speak of life as a fate.

So the vision of human destiny is indeed fundamental. Most twentieth-century researches have drawn attention to the role of early childhood, the environment, and consciousness as the determinants of our respective pathways. These dimensions are certainly important, but they need to be integrated with the silent region, the familial unconscious. For only when we consider life as a whole can we begin to glimpse the strange and mysterious pattern we call destiny.

II. The Theory of the Cain Complex

The following chapters, however, will not be a technical exposition of medical genetics. The psychiatric materials will occupy the background and only become explicit in chapter four. The major endeavor of this book is to interpret the Cain complex. Of all the contributions of Leopold Szondi, this idea is the most creative for theology. The Cain complex is as central to destiny analysis as the Oedipus complex is to psychoanalysis. Whereas the latter is defined as the son who loves the mother and hates the father, the former consists of the son who loves the father and hates the brother.

In recent years the Oedipus formula has been influential in the so-called radical theologies. It takes little imagination to realize that the Oedipal struggle against the father, when projected onto an ultimate level, becomes the human overthrow of God. The attention given to this motif grows out of Freud's belief that the three greatest masterpieces of world literature are concerned with the murder of the father. The three are **Antigone**, **Hamlet**, and **The Brothers Karamazov**.

For some unknown reason Freud and his heirs have neglected an equally important masterpiece--the Bible. The Hebrew tradition is not preoccupied with the murder but with the respect of the father. In Israel the murder of the brother, whether near or far away, whether individual or collective, is more fundamental. The Cain complex is a formula that addresses ordinary family problems and also opens up new areas of investigation.

So this book functions in effect as a theological exposition of the Cain complex. Drawing together materials in religion, psychiatry, and history, the style is interpretive rather than technically exegetical. The major theological thesis is that (1) the origins of good and evil derive from the same biological root, that (2) they may both be subsumed under the doctrine of Creation, and that (3) the old doctrine of the Fall is too simple and no longer necessary. This thesis will begin to be expounded in chapter one but preceded by a brief look at Szondi himself.

III. A Biographical Note

Leopold Szondi was born in a small Hungarian village in 1893. His father, a shoemaker, had thirteen children. Leopold was number twelve. In 1898 the elder Szondi moved his family to Budapest, so his children could be educated. It was at the University of Budapest that Szondi earned his medical degree, became a professor of biology, and received training in psychoanalysis. In his early career he conducted wide ranging research into medical and biological problems, chiefly epilepsy and diseases of the nervous system. Eventually he became one of the most distinguished scientists of Eastern Europe, earning a reputation as a daring investigator, an original thinker, and a dramatic orator. One of his collaborators has said it was a privilege to belong to the Szondi circle in Budapest.(6)

During the 1930's Szondi worked on the boundary line between biology and psychology. He became interested in the psychology of marriage choice after observing familial patterns among his patients. In 1937 he published a now classic essay which demonstrates that marriage attraction grows out of similar or identical genetic patterns.(7) With this publication he introduced the idea of the familial unconscious and began what we now know broadly as family therapy.

His research, however, was interrupted by the outbreak of world war two and the Nazi incursion into Hungary. We Americans are by now acquainted with the great scholars and scientists who emigrated to our shores. The names of Einstein, Goldstein, Tillich, and countless others have entered into the various fields of modern knowledge. But what we often overlook is that equally great scientists like Szondi remained in Europe. So many of their contributions have been somewhat overshadowed by the overly specialized and pragmatic pursuits of American researchers.(8)   And still others perished in the nightmare of the Nazi concentration camps.

Szondi survived the Holocaust and entered into exile in Zürich. It was during the post-war period, particularly between 1944 and 1963, that he wrote his major works. In these years he achieved a highly original blend of genetics, diagnosis, pathology, ego psychology, and psychotherapy. All of these works carry on the motif of destiny. None is now available in English, but translations are in progress.(9)

In the 1960's he turned his attention to the problems of ethics and religion. In 1969 he published his powerful and original study of Cain, followed by an equally significant work on Moses four years later. Both of these volumes expound the Cain complex and offer a profound understanding of the Bible. Neither has been translated into English. However, the Cain complex was presented by me to American readers in the fall of 1979.(10)

In February, 1980 Szondi published a major volume on the theory of aggression. He continues work on the second edition of the Moses. After many years of profound and original research, he stands as one of the great intellectual giants of the present century. My hope in writing this book is that we may gain a new way of looking at ourselves by listening to this master from Budapest.

Footnotes

1.   Leonard Hayflick, "The Cell Biology of Human Aging," Scientific American (Jan., 1980), p. 60.

2.   Cicely Saunders, "Dying They Live," New Meanings of Death, ed. by H. Feifel (New York: McGraw-Hill, 1977), p. 154.

3.   Russell Noyes, "The Experience of Dying," Psychiatry, 35:2 (May, 1972), p. 179.

4.   Leon Wurmser, "Die Bedeutung L. Szondi's für die Psychiatrie," Festschrift Leopold Szondi, ed. by L. Poljak (Bern: Hans Huber, 1963), p. 325.

5.   Aubrey Milunsky, **Know Your Genes** (Boston: Houghton Mifflin, 1977), p. 79.

6.   Interview with Vera Roboz at the University of Navarre, Pamplona, Spain, on August 30, 1978.

7.   L. Szondi, "An Attempt at a Theory of Choice in Love," **Acta Psychologica**, III:1 (1937), pp. 1-80.

8.   Interview with Maurice Bairy at Sophia University, Tokyo, Japan on July 17, 1974.

9.   Szondi's translator is Dietrich Blumer of the University of Michigan Medical School.

10.   Cf. my essay, "Szondi's Theory of the Cain Complex," **American Imago**, 36:3 (Fall, 1979), pp. 260-274.

Chapter One: CREATION AND THE HUMAN ORDER

I.   The Primordial Fire

Before the universe was born, there was nothing but immense and silent void.   The emptiness was endless and dark.   At some point, which we cannot determine, hydrogen, helium, and dust collected into a gigantic ball.   The hydrogen and helium intermingled, rising to a temperature of twenty million degrees. Transformed by such a high intensity, the gaseous ball of particles ignited and exploded, releasing massive waves of fire and light.

The molten fires expanded like a balloon for a billion years until, beginning to move more slowly, they gradually cooled and congealed into huge bodies of matter.   These congealed gasses were distributed in clusters around the void, becoming what we now know as stars and galaxies.   A local group of planetary bodies became the Milky Way, within which our earth would be born.

Our universe exploded into being about twenty billion years ago.(1)   The effects of the primordial explosion still linger as background radiation within the cosmos and at the interior of the earth.   Eventually radioactive elements, buried within our planet, heated up, boiled over, and spilled out as blazing matter onto the craggy surface, forming mountains and valleys.(2)   As these elements boiled out, they vented vapor into the atmosphere where it condensed as moisture and fell back to the ground as rain.   The rains continued until the waters filled up the gigantic valleys of the earth, thus forming the oceans and rivers.

These primeval seas were rich with hydrogen, ammonia, and methane.(3)   Lightning flashes ignited these elements and caused them to form clusters. These were new patterns, containing amino acids and nucleotides, and, when combined with one another, could produce a self-copying molecule.   This has been called DNA by modern science; for it contains the fundamental structure of life--the ability to replicate itself.   The tiny DNA molecule is shaped like a zipper.   It unzips, producing two strands, and they, in turn, unzip again and again.   In this way, from the archaic beginnings, the smaller elements of the cosmos have for millions of years reproduced themselves.

1

The formation and reformation of minute nucleotide patterns continued until the ancient seas were teeming with life. Modern science teaches us that originally all life arose from water. A succession of animal forms made the treacherous journey from the sea to the land. First amphibious creatures, then reptilian, and much later mammals arose to dominance on the land. But the conquest of earth could not have been possible without a precious chemical--oxygen. The triumphant march from the sea was so full of danger and the threat of suffocation so great that only oxygen bearing plants saved the primeval creatures from extinction. The presence of oxygen was correlated with the drive of life toward more complex systems of respiration. So when archaic creatures settled permanently upon the land, they could do it only with the breath of life.

By now this scientific theory of the origins of the universe has become well known. As students of Christian theology, we should understand and appreciate this account because it sets forth an age-old claim of religious belief--that the world has an origin, a limit, beyond which we cannot penetrate. In scientific terms the universe is created in chance.(4) The appeal to chance is welcome to theology; for it prevents us from reducing the beginning to a simple cause-effect process. The beginning is enshrouded in an ultimate mystery.

A theory of the universe is even useful to a theological understanding of human destiny. First, science confirms that all life is interrelated. Between the primordial fire blast and the present organization of matter and energy there is no gap. The interval consists of slow, cumulative time, and most of this can be known by scientific investigation. The structures of the cosmos can be described mathematically and formulated in terms of law. Two basic laws are those of symmetry and the conservation of energy.(5) These are conservative postulates which tell us that the forms of life seek to preserve their essential characteristics.

Second, living beings develop internally and irreversibly. As soon as a human being is born, he or she receives a design of a relative span of life.(6) The length of the life span is directly proportionate to the number of times a cell replicates itself in the body. The allotment functions as a blueprint for the

2

unfolding of a destiny. The blueprint includes other genetic information, such as hair color, eye color, bodily shape, and disease potentiality. In the course of life, as the individual interacts with others, one is inclined to move forward in a single direction, unless disturbed by a pathology. Irreversibility is an essential characteristic of interacting organisms.(7)

These two ideas stipulate that the world is relational, life developmental. The decisions made by self-conscious beings carry out a fundamental life plan. The combination of choosing and receiving, of going forth and carrying on is the secret of human destiny. No matter how hard we try, we cannot escape our connection to archaic nature. The human-nature bond is inseparably formed by the fact that our DNA code is the same as that of animals, and the chemistry of our blood has the same saline ingredients of the primeval seas. Just as the universe comes into being in fire, so does each human life come out of an ecstatic union of mother and father.

In as much as mankind and nature are one, we may posit a fundamental psychological principle: the law of participation.(8) This means that the basic tendency of all human life is to establish relationships within nature and to transcend it. For mankind walks on a boundary line between the most refined self-consciousness and the most inert instinctual mechanisms, between culture and nature. How we make our passage on that boundary line is the critical problem of human destiny.

II. Creation and Destiny

In current cosmology the universe, having exploded into being, is now moving more and more slowly. The expanding balloon will one day lose its energy and collapse upon itself. The great galaxies clustered on the surface will crash into a nothingness, returning to the primeval void before the beginning. From the fire shall come the ashes.

There is a certain frustration among scientists when they consider this theory. For they like to push the sequence of cause and effect backward without limit. But the failure to go behind the so-called "Big Bang" tends to be satisfying to religious believers. Although this cosmology does not support a

3

simple theism, it does correspond to a religious vision of human destiny as originally told in the book of Genesis.

The main intent of Genesis chapter one is to proclaim a transcendent God. God envelops the world as an abyss of darkness yet remains beyond it in majesty and awe. Still the faith of biblical peoples attests that God is knowable in particular disclosures. He is primordial and relational. For this reason it is difficult to say that God is "before" the world or "beyond" it. The forms of space and time are ways of organizing our practical experience, and they are secondary in any fundamental analysis of reality.

In modern times the German mystic Jacob Boehme perhaps has come the closest in understanding the mysterious God-world relation.(9) He envisaged an ultimate abyss of darkness and nothingness, out of which a primordial fire has ignited the universe. He named the abyss the Ungrund, a German term referring to a groundless nothingness yet alive with explosive energy. The darkness comes out of the Godhead and is the source of the fire that exploded the world into being. The planets took shape as the elements of the fire congealed and cooled into living matter. Though the Creation occurred long ago, the fiery radiation still lingers in the cosmos as an ever-present realm of creation and destruction.

The biblical parallel to the nothingness is simpler but just as dramatic. In Genesis chapter one, the earth is empty before the Creation. "The earth was without form and void, and darkness was upon the face of the deep; and the Spirit of God was moving over the face of the waters." (Gen. 1:2) The void symbolizes the primal nakedness of the world. It is superseded but not annulled by the Creation.

Unlike modern science the Bible does not try to quantify nature. By using simple pastoral images, Genesis nevertheless sets forth a deep insight into the relation of God, nature, and mankind. Living beings occupy their respective spheres according to their ability to move. Earth, water, and firmament stand in relation to each other. Since the Bible subordinates Creation to God, it represents the relativity of things. Space and time are not basic but rather attributes of divine activity.(10)

4

The climax of Creation, however, comes with the appearance of mankind. Man and woman are blessed and awarded dominion over the face of the earth. "Be fruitful and multiply, and fill the earth and subdue it; and have dominion over the fish of the sea and over the birds of the air and over every living thing that moves upon the earth." (Gen. 1:28) In recent years scientists have expressed their fears that this passage exalts a human exploitation of limited natural resources and beauty.

But verse 28 only makes sense when connected with what follows it. "Behold, I have given you every plant yielding seed which is upon the face of all the earth, and every tree with seed in its fruit; you shall have them for food." (Gen. 1:29) As modern science knows, plants give oxygen that fills human lungs, allowing male and female of all ages to stand up and live. Without plants we could neither eat nor breathe. So we should ask how could we possibly exploit the earth when we are dependent upon it for breath?

The Bible does not sanction exploitation but recommends a responsible interaction with the plant and animal kingdoms. The Scriptures have a crucial concept which gives us the logic of human destiny in relation to nature. This idea has been called the "act-fate" sequence. It is as important to the moral order of the world as the genetic code is to the bio-chemical. Unless we understand the act-fate structure of human experience, we cannot formulate a biblically based and scientifically sound theory of destiny.

Every action, whether good or bad, has an effect. Every action creates a series of consequences that reverberate in three directions: outward to all others, onward to future times and places, and backward to the actor. The consequences with their diverse vibrations form a partly conscious, partly unconscious sphere of moral worth within human communities. (11) These consequences influence us and press us to make particular kinds of decisions which may not be commensurate with the original intent, since the effects are open-ended and unpredictable. This simple formula reminds us that nothing happens in isolation and that good acts do not automatically lead to good consequences. The moral effects may even bear a mixture of good and evil.

The act-fate sequence helps us to understand what is meant by the "image of God," in which man and woman are created. That the image includes an irreducibly unique dimension of freedom has been recognized by Christian tradition. In contrast to the Eastern Church, Protestantism has emphasized that the image includes both the ability to act and to relate, hence to be free and have a destiny. With this insight Protestant theology has declared that the Eastern distinction between the image and the likeness of God, that is, freedom and communion, is not necessary. The image includes both freedom and communion, because all human action is relational.

Such a relational freedom becomes real when God "formed man of dust from the ground, and breathed into his nostrils the breath of life; and man became a living being." (Gen. 2:7) The divine Spirit animates what is essentially a finite frame. This does not contradict the scientific account but provides a way to understand that the basis of human existence is dependence upon nature, such as oxygen from plants, and yet participation in an ultimate relation. The Creation story makes the human creature a free but finite being who observes the law of participation.

The profound insight in verse seven is that the basis of human life is derivative. In as much as the breath of life is given, it may also be taken away.(12) That the breath of life may be withdrawn means that a natural death is interwoven into human nature from the beginning. Life and death are one wherever men and women dwell. This does not specify how they will die; for dying differs from death as such. So while Genesis chapter two fails to spell out the conditions for human dying, it does account for natural death.

Born with the dual possibility of life and death, man and woman are set in the garden, in Eden. Arriving in the garden is the beginning of human destiny; for the occupants are commanded to cultivate the ground and name the animals. The command stipulates the making of a vocational decision and presupposes the development of mental and contact modes of activity. The man and woman, or Adam and Eve, are also married. We may even assume that they enjoy a sexual union while in Eden. For the definition of marriage denotes a physical union: "Therefore a man leaves his father and his mother and cleaves to his wife, and they become one flesh." (Gen. 2:24)

6

III. The Ancestral Legacy

Although Genesis exalts the mystery of flesh, it has become the task of modern science to lay bare the basic factors of human nature. Both science and the Bible teach the complementarity of the human and animal kingdoms. We are dependent upon nature and yet, in our freedom, we transcend it. Though we stand out from nature, its functions always remain in our background as real potentialities.

The research into the biological aspect of human nature is still in progress and remains somewhat controversial. It is a mistake to look upon animal studies in terms of a simple doctrine of evolution. These investigations illumine what is given innately in human behavior. If humans and animals share the same function, then it probably informs us as a natural endowment. But this does not mean that animals cause human characteristics.

The correlation of human and animal functions points to behavior as a matter of inclination rather than conditioning.(13) The idea of inclination also appears in classical Thomistic theology. An inclination is psychologically understood as a motivating drive, containing a complex set of needs and tendencies. A drive is hereditary, but it is also shaped by learning.

Of the contemporary positions, destiny analysis seems to have the most comprehensive and accurate theory of drives. In Szondian psychiatry each drive comprises two complementary needs. The purpose of each need is to regulate the other in a dynamic equilibrium and build up the drive. Each need consists of two contrary tendencies, one positive, one negative. The same needs and tendencies are in all persons as potentialities by biological descent.

But no person acts out all of the needs at the same time. Individual differences in heredity, learned, and traumatic behavior compel some tendencies to become dominant, while the others occupy the background. Unlike animals, our needs and tendencies are not fixed at birth; we must develop and combine them in culture. For human destiny is a fluid pattern, bearing complex possibilities, free and unfree choices. Whatever way our destiny takes, it will proceed through the following drives:

A.   The Contact Drive.   Human experience is fundamentally relational.   The contact drive propels people to find objects and relate to them.(14)   This inclination is the basis of language, culture, and all caring behavior.   Many theorists overlook the contact drive and naively identify its functions with sexuality.   But contact is an independent pattern consisting of two needs.

1.   The Need for Acceptance.   After the separation from the mother by birth, the child experiences a life-long need for acceptance and attachment.   This is originally satisfied by a fulfilling relationship with the mother, then the father and the family.   Unless the infancy relation is warm and secure, the child will lack a basic acceptance until death.   This need revolves around two hereditary tendencies.

(a.)   Bonding.   All children have an innate tendency to hang on to the mother for protection, nourishment, and acceptance.   This tendency toward parental care is genetically encoded.(15)   Bonding is visible in the grasping reflexes of babies, their oral attachments to the mother's breast, and sleeping in fetal positions.   In later infancy it comes out in finger sucking.   These movements manifest the erogeneity of the hand which we share with other primates.

(b.)   Separating.   The opposite tendency is being alone, and it is equally significant in the natural desire for solitude.   An early death of the parent can activate this tendency negatively and further heighten the need for acceptance.

2.   The Need for Acquisition.   The other half of the contact drive is to leave the family and early childhood in order to search for new objects and broader experiences.

(a.)   Seeking.   This need is propelled by the natural tendency to seek new relations as substitutes for the parental bond.   Seeking together with bonding are the two positive tendencies at work in normal interpersonal and cultural life.

(b.)   Clinging.   But the negative tendency of holding on to the past comes out on occasion, particularly when we lack self-acceptance and simply hang on to a lost relationship.   The failure to acquire new

8

experiences, following a trauma for example, leads to a disintegration of the contact drive. Common forms of disintegration are depression, frustration, incestuous clinging, and their opposite--restless mania. In depression, the two needs split, while the clinging and the bonding come together. Thus, the essence of depression is not loss as such, but the clinging to a lost relation.

B. **The Sexual Drive.** Though rarely used to form bonds among animals, sex may influence contact-seeking. Mainly sexuality is active in self-preservation and procreation for humans and animals. Sexuality has two needs.

1. **The Need for Tenderness.** This is an individualized love expressed toward another person regardless of gender.

(a.) **Personal Love.** The tenderness may be directed toward a specific person.

(b.) **Collective Love.** Or it may be sublimated toward a group in a general altruism.

2. **The Need for Aggression.** Complete human sexuality also includes aggression. Love and aggression together provide ecstasy in the sex act. Aggression is correlated with the sexual hormone and the nucleus amygdala in the limbic system of the brain.

(a.) **Active Aggression.** The need reflects a tendency to dominate a partner or opponent in an experience of pleasure.

(b.) **Passive Aggression.** The other tendency is to re-direct the aggression against oneself. In normal experience this often works with the tendency toward collective love in a de-sexualized general altruism.

When there is a disturbance of the sexual drive, the two needs split and their respective opposite tendencies become co-active. In an advanced state such disintegration comes out as sadism and masochism. These pathologies really enhance the two opposite needs, often in great erotic and aggressive activity, which are sometimes hard to control.

C. The Paroxysmal Drive. One of the contributions of animal studies is the discovery that a strong
emotion like hatred differs from aggression.(16)
Emotions are energy responses originating in the old
mammalian startle pattern. Humans inherit this innate
function of reacting with a surprise in defense
against a threat. Whereas animals face external
dangers, humans confront inner and outer crises. In
human behavior the startle and the discharge of
primitive emotions are united in the same drive.(17)

1. The Need for Restitution. One half of human
paroxysmality is the need to make amends for an
explosion of violent emotions. Once the passions are
released, the organism seeks to re-balance itself and
reinstate a previous condition.

(a.) The Abel Tendency. The cyclical restitution activates such refined emotions as goodness,
justice, tolerance, courage, and harmony.

(b.) The Cain Tendency. These emotions are the
polar opposite of rage and hatred, envy and jealousy,
anger and vengeance. The latter are coarse affects
discharged in the struggle against danger. The only
difference between the two tendencies is a qualitative
release of energy. Otherwise they are both rooted in
the same source. Chapter three will explain the
dialectic of these emotions, for they lie at the heart
of the Cain complex.

2. The Need for Value. The other half of the
paroxysmal drive is the need to manifest moral worth
in human communities. Usually this is attested in the
eyes of other people.

(a.) Self-Display. The moral need shows a
tendency to assert oneself, to claim one's own worth.
But this can become arrogance or exhibitionism.

(b.) Self-Concealment. The opposite is the
inclination to hide oneself, particularly in the
presence of danger. It is present in shyness, guilt,
the fear of punishment, shame, and anxiety. The
purpose of this side is to activate the movement
toward restitution after a discharge of the Cain
affects.

The paroxysmal drive is also correlated with the
limbic system. This has been confirmed in studies of

epilepsy.(18) Clinically, the Cain emotions are related to epilepsy, because both are shock events. The Abel-Cain pattern is complemented by the need for value, and the latter corresponds to the medical category of hysteroid ailments. The reason is that a shock of rage or hatred activates anxiety or guilt. The Cain emotions also represent the concept of the irascible in classical theology, while the Abel convey that of the concupiscable.(19)

In times of great danger, the paroxysmal drive can break down into two advanced forms. One is the model of evil, the pure Cain, consisting of the respective emotions and the exhibitionism. The other is the good, the pure Abel, involving the positive emotions and the tendency to hide oneself. Chapter four will illustrate the Abel syndrome in the destiny of Moses.

D. The Ego. What separates mankind from the animal kingdom is a larger, more complex brain-mind system. The brain, with its two cerebral hemispheres, is correlated with the mind or self-consciousness. The brain-mind system permits us to speak of an ego as a principle of personal identity. The ego is not identified with a specific function or located in a single organ. Rather the ego is a mode of acting and relating, the seat of decision-making roughly midway between the conscious and unconscious domains. The task of the ego is to make the decisions to unfold a destiny.

1. The Imagination. One side of the ego is creative and expansive. It may use such clinical mechanisms as projection and inflation in the formulation of ideas, concepts, and a sense of being. But the imaginative aspect of the ego is also vulnerable to disintegration in the various kinds of schizophrenia.

2. The Will. The ego exercises choice, and it controls the upsurge of sexual desires and primitive Cain emotions. The will is not an independent clinical entity. It is an act involving perception, memory, and the mechanisms of adaptation, such as introjection, denial, and repression. In times of illness, the will may disintegrate in the form of inhibition, suicide, or destruction.

11

All of these drives are bequeathed to us by nature. Some of the tendencies become dominant, some hidden. Some will be chosen, some repressed. Rarely will all the needs and tendencies come out, because our passage is mysterious and changing.

In Genesis chapter two Adam and Eve stand at the pinnacle of Creation. Endowed with the contact and sexual drives, will and imagination, they are the jewels of God's handiwork. But so far in the story, something is missing. They have met no danger, wrestled with no crises, and conquered no obstacles. So Adam and Eve, in the hour of their creation, are waiting for an unknown danger. For they have yet to face their mysterious paroxysmal natures.

Footnotes

1. Robert Jastrow, **Until the Sun Dies** (New York: Norton, 1977), p. 21.

2. Preston Cloud, **Cosmos, Earth, and Man** (New Haven: Yale, 1978), p. 117.

3. Alexander Oparin, **The Chemical Origin of Life**, trans. by A. Synge (Springfield: Charles C. Thomas, 1964), p. 32.

4. Jacques Monod, **Le Hasard et La Necessite** (Paris: Editions du Seuil, 1970), p. 112.

5. Richard Feynman, **The Character of Physical Law** (Cambridge: M. I. T., 1965), pp. 85-104.

6. Aubrey Milunsky, **Know Your Genes**, p. 271.

7. Feynman, op.cit., p. 113.

8. L. Szondi, **Ich-Analyse** (Bern: Hans Huber, 1956), p. 35.

9. Alexandre Koyre, **La Philosophie de Jacob Boehme** (New York: Burt Franklin, 1968), pp. 322-326.

10. Max Jammer, **Concepts of Space** (Cambridge: Harvard, 1969), p. 23.

11. Klaus Koch, "The Old Testament View of Nature," **Anticipation**, 25 (Jan., 1979), p. 50; "Gibt

es ein Vergeltungsdogma im Alten Testament?"
Zeitschrift für Theologie und Kirche, LII (1955), p.
32.

12. Edmond Jacob, Theology of the Old Testament,
trans. by A. Heathcote and P. Allcock (New York:
Harper, 1958), p. 160.

13. Irenäus Eibl-Eibesfeldt, Love and Hate,
trans. by G. Strachan (New York: Schocken, 1974), p.
5.

14. L. Szondi, Die Triebentmischten (Bern: Hans
Huber, 1980), p. 251.

15. Theodosius Dobzhansky, The Biology of
Ultimate Concern (New York: Meridian, 1967), p. 85.

16. Konrad Lorenz, On Aggression, trans. by M.
Wilson (New York: Harcourt, Brace & World, 1966), p.
217.

17. L. Szondi, Lehrbuch des Experimentellen
Triebdiagnostik (Bern: Hans Huber, 1960), pp. 101-
103.

18. Paul MacLean, A Triune Concept of the Brain
and Behavior (Toronto: University of Toronto, 1973),
pp. 23-31.

19. Thomas Aquinas, Summa Theologica, Quest. 23,
Pts. 1-2, Arts. I, II.

Chapter Two: THE ORIGIN OF GOOD AND EVIL

I. The Primeval Crisis

The biblical story of Creation is unique because
it connects the ethical order of human experience with
the origin of the world. The potentiality to act in
good or evil ways is given in the beginning, transmitted in biological descent, and manifest in the crises
of experience. As we have seen, Adam and Eve are
endowed with mental, relational, and sexual abilities.
Their destiny has already begun in their marriage to
each other and in their confrontation with the environment. But their destiny has not yet taken on any
moral significance, because they have not faced any
crises.

The task of Genesis chapter three is to narrate
how Adam and Eve acquire a distinctly moral consciousness. In order for them to think and act ethically
they must experience conflict. This drama begins when
God imposes a command. "You may freely eat of every
tree of the garden; but of the tree of the knowledge
of good and evil you shall not eat, for in the day
that you eat of it you shall die." (Gen. 2:16b-17)

Placing a taboo on a part of the Creation seems
slightly strange, since God has already declared it to
be good. (Gen. 1:31) The text does not say why God
sets forth the command. What appears to be confusing
is that dying would be the consequence of eating the
fruit. The command, while referring to a mode of
dying, cannot refer to death as such. For natural
death is already present as a correlate of life.

The scene becomes even more complicated when the
serpent enters and announces: "Did God say, 'You
shall not eat of any tree of the garden'?" (Gen. 3:1b)
After summarizing God's taboo, the snake then speaks
in a strange, haunting way: "You will not die. For
God knows that when you eat of it your eyes will be
opened, and you will be like God, knowing good and
evil." (Gen. 3:4b-5) The key is what the serpent
says. It contradicts God and thereby introduces an
enormous threat, a possibility of imminent, mortal
danger.

Eve is the first to respond to the crisis. "So
when the woman saw that the tree was good for food,
and that it was a delight to the eyes, and that the

15

tree was to be desired (chamad) to make one wise ...."
(Gen. 3:6a) Keeping in mind that Eve is now trying to
resolve a crisis of great danger, how shall we understand her arousal of feeling? In as much as the
Hebrew verb speaks of the desire for wisdom, then we
are not dealing with a sexual arousal. It is more
precisely a moral arousal, a fascination for the value
of wisdom, an ecstatic vision of an awesome new worth.

We can get a clue to what Eve might have felt
when we consult a classic medical description of those
faced with similar mortal danger.

> There was no anxiety, no trace of despair,
> no pain; but rather calm seriousness,
> profound acceptance, and a dominant mental
> quickness and sense of surety. Mental
> activity became enormous, rising to a
> hundred-fold velocity or intensity. The
> relationships of events and their probable
> outcomes were overviewed with objective
> clarity.(1)

The desire for the knowledge of good and evil, as
Gerhard von Rad has shown, is a drive to achieve a
comprehensive knowledge.(2) In the light of this
clinical quotation, may we not infer that Eve felt an
accelerated mental and moral power in her quest for a
resolution of the conflict?

But with penetrating insight the story observes
that Eve gave some fruit to her husband, and they both
enjoyed it. "Then the eyes of both were opened, and
they knew that they were naked ...." (Gen. 3:7a) In
the aftermath of a quickened thinking and feeling
state, they achieve a new insight and a sense of
shame. Contrary to what we commonly assume, it is a
mistake to interpret the shame as a sexual feeling.
Indeed shame is a moral sentiment, a tendency to
conceal one's face from the eyes of others. It is a
natural defense against an inordinate display of
oneself in the same way that one feels apologetic
after performing an outstanding feat.

Along with the shame, Adam and Eve feel an over-
powering sense of fear. They shudder, wrap themselves
with aprons made of fig leaves, run away, and hide.
But the shame, the fear, and the flight are all of the
same pattern, a hysteroid defense against danger,
which is a natural correlate of the original fascina-

tion. They continue to tremble until evening, when God strolls through the garden and discovers that they are aware of their nakedness and afraid. God asks how Adam could know he were naked and afraid--unless he had broken the taboo. Adam quickly confesses his misdeed. But he says that Eve made him do it. She in turn blames the serpent.

The sequence of blaming each other is an example of what we call, in modern terms, a projection. Unable to tolerate the surge of fear and shame, Adam and Eve transfer these feelings onto the snake. There is nothing unusual about this, since we all use projection as an initial defense against the sudden upsurge of primitive emotions. But the profound significance of the projection is that now Adam and Eve possess an inner sense of danger. How, we should ask, is such a feeling possible? Must there not be something already latent in Adam and Eve, enabling them to feel the danger as well as the moral arousal?

They can only have these experiences if they already possess an unconscious image of death. To be capable of ecstasy, to stand outside of oneself, requires that one already have a deep and latent acquaintance with separation. There is only one source for this condition--when Adam and Eve are first created by the breath of God. The breath separates them from the earth and thereby inserts a latent acquaintance with death.

So when God threatens Adam and Eve with a possible dying, he is not introducing death as a new possibility. Death is present from the beginning. In fact, the serpent simply clarifies the situation to mean: You will not be struck down now. It is the threat that touches down to the latent awareness of mortality, lifting them to the heights of ecstasy.

But coping with the crisis is not simply an external condition of morality. It must be internal. The story goes on to show how an inner conflict will be a permanent feature of human existence as a prerequisite for a moral consciousness. God announces that Adam, and all subsequent men, will inherit a life of anguish and labor. Eve and women will suffer painful childbirth. The snake will cease to be upright and four-legged, becoming a crawler. Their existence will climax with a return to the dust. (Gen. 3:19b)

17

God's declaration is not so much a curse as it is an acknowledgment of finite existence.(3) Similarly, there is nothing unnatural in the fate of Adam, Eve, and the serpent. In biology, it is held that reptiles have evolved from four-legged creatures to crawlers, and women have had painful childbirths because humans are upright and possessed with an increased brain size.(4) That men have had to struggle for existence is a part of the human epic.

Chapter three concludes with a startling confession by God. "Behold, the man has become like one of us, knowing good and evil; and now, lest he put forth his hand and take also of the tree of life, and eat, and live forever." (Gen. 3:22) We should read this in the sense that God has either permitted us to become morally experienced or that he has expected it. But though we humans have achieved great moral and mental power, we shall not become immortal. We are only permitted to be morally aware. Therefore, we like Adam and Eve, should go on our way. We cannot return to the garden, because the entrance is blocked with an angel wielding a flaming sword.

Influenced by classical theology and psychoanalysis, many interpreters have seen in chapter three a family drama. Describing God as a stern father figure, they have interpreted Eve's and Adam's action as disobedience or rebellion. In a dogmatic sense disobedience merits punishment in the Fall and exile from the garden. To a secular observer the action might be understood as a rebellion from God like that of the Greek Prometheus.

They are surely correct in addressing the context as familial. It is a mistake to regard the action in chapter three as individualistic. But in view of verse 22 it is equally misleading to emphasize disobedience. Rather it appears that God himself creates the crisis, or at least tolerates it, in order that the couple might develop. This corresponds to what Reformed theologians have sometimes called a "permission to sin." However, Adam and Eve are not committing a sin in a simple manner. They are experiencing fascination and mental exhilaration which are prerequisites for both good and evil.

We can get a sharper insight by borrowing an idea from contemporary family therapists. It has been said that there actually is no adolescent rebellion in any

18

family. The alleged disobedience is, at a deeper level, action approved by the parent. The child is either acting out what the parent has done or unconsciously would like to do. In this way the child becomes a delegate for the parent.(5) With reference to Genesis chapter three, we could easily say that Eve is a delegate for God. By accomplishing the moral breakthrough she actually carries out what God wishes.

Therefore, chapter three heralds--it seems to me--not disobedience but a delegation of power. This means that the exile is fully expected as a natural consequence of suddenly growing up. On leaving the garden, Adam and Eve set out on a moral mission conducted with a loyalty to the "father." They are obliged to work, which entails a vocational decision. This is their second fateful decision, the first being their marriage. Sadly they look forward to a hastened death which will complete their destiny. For dying, or what we now call accident proneness, can occur more readily in a life lived with strong emotion. This connection between emotion and dying is also an implication of God's original taboo.

Since the episode is conducted in emotion, including the fascination and fear, it is not a matter of sexuality. The tendency of traditional interpreters, both theological and psychoanalytic, to make sexuality fundamental in this story is misleading. Sexuality is simply instrumental in procreating the next generation. Rather, chapter three indicates that the paroxysmal drive is being triggered through its latent hysteroid side. In its clinical form the paroxysmal-hysteroid pattern unfolds in three stages: (1) seizure of the consciousness in a desire for values; (2) numbness by fear, shyness, or shame; and (3) restitution in the form of neurotic symptoms or estrangement.(6)

We therefore cannot say that Adam and Eve have sinned in the fullest sense. But we must admit that what they have accomplished is a prelude to a far more catastrophic situation among their offspring.

II. The Tragedy of Cain

After leaving the garden, Adam and Eve decide to expand their family. Eve gives birth to two sons, Cain and Abel. Cain grows up to be a farmer, Abel a shepherd. As the eldest, Cain should be the privileged son. In accord with custom both sons offer the fruit of their work to God. With a stunning surprise God accepts Abel's but rejects Cain's. The eldest son of Adam becomes enraged. For by his position in the family his sacrifice should have been chosen.

Generations of biblical scholars have tried to explain why God acted in this way. The text does not reveal God's motive. One common explanation is that God prefers blood sacrifices, which would have occurred, assuming Abel offered a lamb. This hypothesis reduces the story to a reflection of cultic practice, thus narrowing the claim for universality as befits a doctrine of Creation. These opening chapters of Genesis articulate truths which are valid at any time and place.

Consequently, the position of Martin Buber seems the most accurate. God is simply testing Cain and his family.(7) This is not the same as a temptation or a leading into evil. Rather it is an attempt to make a crisis, so that Cain can cope with it and thereby enlarge his own moral capacity. This implies that God rejects Cain's offering for the same reason that he has originally tabooed the tree of knowledge.

What is significant is how Cain reacts. He "was very angry, and his countenance fell." (Gen. 4:5b) He incurred a primitive emotion and a demolished self image. But he became neither sadistic, depressed, nor psychotic. We must ask where did Cain get his tendency to handle crises emotionally? There can only be one answer--from his parents. He reacts the same way his mother and father did, when confronted with their crisis. The major difference is that they released more refined emotions. Cain's feelings are more crude, coarse, and primitive.

God is deeply concerned about Cain and admonishes him. "Why are you angry, and why has your countenance fallen? If you do well, will you not be accepted? And if you do not do well, sin is crouching at the door; its desire is for you, but you must master it." (Gen. 4:6b-7) This is the first explicit reference to sin. Cain is allowed to choose a destiny based upon sin or upon an acceptance of God's mysterious ways. He faces a terrible choice of a creative destiny or a crippling fate.

God hopes that Cain will master the conflict. But Cain suffers too much. So he accompanies Abel into the wilderness and slays him. The implication is that Cain murders his brother in rage and envy.

In preserving this story the Hebrew tradition has added additional insights into the motive of the crime. Both brothers are married. Rabbinic tradition teaches that Abel's wife is more beautiful than Cain's.(8) So Cain murders out of jealousy and greed. He wants to possess Abel's wife in order to enhance his power and overcome his threatened position in the family. If so, then the jealousy and envy are psychologically the same as rage and anger. They are crude epileptoid emotions co-acting with an aroused sexual drive, interpersonal isolation, and a defeated ego.

Since the two brothers are married, who are their wives? With no other families present, they can only be their sisters. This means that Adam tolerates incest in his family. This also conflicts with classical psychoanalysis which holds that the incest taboo is universal. If this were true, then Cain's murder of Abel would be an attempt to slay a substitute for his father Adam in order to possess his mother Eve, a pattern that conforms to that of the Oedipus complex. But in contrast to the psychoanalytic view, Cain only hates his brother. He loves his parents and God.

The issue in the Cain story is not one of sexual conflict. By looking at the family biologically, we can understand how the incest fits into the story. When families engage in inbreeding, they risk not only social isolation but also the probability that latent lethal tendencies will become manifest in the offspring. Since Cain has chosen homicidal emotion as a way to cope with crises, then through a narrow gene pool and a tight family tradition, this could become so adaptive as to survive as a pattern in subsequent generations.

After the murder occurs, God looks around for Abel. He confronts Cain as to where his brother Abel might be. "I do not know; am I my brother's keeper?" (Gen. 4:9b) Then in profound and abject anguish God realizes that Abel has been murdered. His blood has spilled onto the earth and cried out for vengeance. The bond between mankind and the earth, established at Creation, has been spoiled. But the act-fate sequence remains intact. Cain is seized with a cyclical rebound of guilt and a dread of punishment. He cries:

> My punishment is greater than I can bear. Behold, thou hast driven me this day away from the ground; and from thy face I shall be hidden; and I shall be a fugitive and a wanderer on the earth, and whoever finds me will slay me. (Gen. 4:13b-14)

Cain trembles in terror. He has committed the first sin and set up a model for evil. For once an experience has taken place, the act-fate structure will preserve it as an ever-present possibility.

Now Cain, guilt-ridden, volatile, and explosive, has to become a vagabond. He can no longer farm the ground. The land has become dangerous, full of insecurity, echoing cries of vengeance. But God intercedes and places a sign of protection upon Cain. Lest anyone slay the eldest son of Adam, God will protect him up to the seventh generation of the family. (Gen. 4:15a) Since the sign, represented in legend as a horn on the forehead, is a prohibition against further violence, it functions as an ethical norm of restitution. God makes atonement by completing the cycle of murder and guilt.

So far, the story has enough accuracy and consistency to permit a clinical and ethical definition. The murder may function as a model of evil, and it consists of the following paroxysmal-epileptoid schema:(9)

1. In reaction to the threat the coarse primitive emotions of rage, hatred, envy, anger, jealousy, and/or vengeance intensify to a lethal peak. Let us call this phase the paroxysmal, these affects the Cain emotions.

2. They explode, seizing the consciousness, possessing one in a helpless, passive twilight state. As the Cain emotions ignite, the cerebral hemispheres are blocked, so that memory and self-consciousness become dysfunctional. This is an epileptoid state, and it is extremely dangerous provided that:

(a.) The ego loses its autonomy and becomes transparent to the fiery Cain passions. The discharge of rage threatens to upset the stability of the ego and so produces anxiety, guilt, fear, or shame. These are a complementary hysteroid reaction, signifying the threat one feels when the primitive paroxysmal drive takes over the self.

(b.) The aggressiveness of the sexual drive is triggered as a co-active force. Herein sexuality mixes with the primary force, the paroxysmal function. This mixture shows that the oldest layers of the brain are totally involved in the commission of evil.

(c.) The relational function is also disrupted during the Cain event. Like Cain himself a murderer tends to be isolated, alienated, or lonely. But alienation by itself cannot lead to murder. Neither can depression, or sexual and mental problems. All of these factors need to be present to enact the Cain event.

3. Finally, as soon as the murder is committed with a foreground paroxysmal-epileptoid seizure, the background hysteroid pattern rotates with an upsurge of anxiety and guilt, fear and shame. This phase causes the organism to re-balance itself in a drive for ethical and biological homeostasis. This is completed with an opening onto a transcendent plane, as demonstrated by Cain's plea to God. The conclusion of the Cain pattern illustrates how fundamental values are in biological nature.

This model represents a hard-core Cain event. It corresponds to what we have known historically as madness. An excellent example of the Cain madness appears unintentionally in one of Rollo May's books. I will emphasize the key Cain references:

How close this rage is to a **temporary psychosis**. As I walk down the street on a sidewalk that seems very **far away**, I cannot think; I am in a **daze**. But it is foggy only externally--inside I am **hyperalive**, hyper-aware of every thought and feeling, as though I am in an **illuminated world**, every-thing very real. The only trouble is that this inner illumination has practically **no connection** with the outside world.

I feel slightly **ashamed** in relation to the outside world--**ashamed** and **defenseless**.

I could understand how, when this state is
relatively permanent, people do themselves
harm, step in front of a motor car for
example. They do this mostly out of a lack
of awareness of the real world about them.
They do it also out of revenge. Or they get
a gun and shoot somebody.(10)

In this confession the elements of the Cain event are
present. But since this man, according to May's
discussion, does not actually commit a murder, we are
led to the question as to how he can live in society
with his Cain emotions.

III. Masking the Cain Complex

Genesis chapter four resumes the story of the
lonely, tragic Cain as he makes his way into the
wilderness. Then he "knew his wife, and she conceived
and bore Enoch; and he built a city, and called the
name of the city after the name of his son, Enoch."
(Gen. 4:17) Building the first city is Cain's
vocational choice, the first fateful decision after
slaying his brother.

Cain's action has provided a way for theologians
to symbolize the nature of the city. Jacques Ellul
has correlated the Cain evil with the city and the
Abel goodness with the country.(11) I disagree with
Ellul when he defines the sign of Cain as a curse and
the building of the city as a defiance of God. What,
we should ask, could Cain do, since he would no longer
be able to farm the land? His vocational choice is
simply a prudent way to socialize his volatile emotional nature. The decision permits us to employ a
psychiatric notion of the complementarity of Cain's
personality. Building the city constitutes his
interpersonal foreground aspect; while his fiery and
explosive emotions lie in the background. The
foreground is therefore a mask for the ancestral
background.

Cain's decision also shows us that even the most
lethal and disturbed among us must live in society.
The observable ways of interaction can be symptomatic
of an underlying Cain conflict. Normally, the Cain
complex takes shape in childhood between ages three
and five, particularly in families with more than one
child. The complex can also be triggered by moral
conflicts between conscience and the environment.

While the complex may lie somewhat dormant during later childhood and adolescence, it frequently appears in young adulthood and remains until old age. Throughout one's life span the Cain predicament may be manifest in a variety of defense mechanisms and neuroses.

Of the neuroses, the most frequent Cain types are obsessional-compulsion, alienation neuroses such as phobias, hypochondria, active anal-sadistic inversion, projective-paranoia, perversions like exhibitionism, and the following psychosomatic complaints: migraines, allergies, bronchial asthma, eczema, angina pectoris, myocardial infarction, high blood pressure, ulcers, intestinal upsets, and diabetes.(12) Many of these presuppose a genetic prediposition toward paroxysmal behavior, and they usually arise in times of crisis and conflict. They are ways of coping without actually killing someone.

Along with the neuroses the Cain complex can be masked through various defense mechanisms. Repression, inhibition, and alienation can be present. But Cain types are more likely to choose two specific kinds of defenses: projection and self-destruction. The first may occur after committing a crime, as one transfers the guilt of the deed onto someone else. The second is more complicated and, on occasion, more radical. Usually it takes three forms.

1. It comes out as a preoccupation with filth, pornography, and obscene gestures. Cain types swear loudly, appear abusive, and enjoy telling dirty jokes.

2. Self-destruction is manifest in explicit suicide tendencies, whether real or imagined. This leads toward wreckless living, taking excessive risks, or engaging in heavy drinking and drug usage.

3. Cain self-destructiveness also comes out in actions that sabotage or undermine one's job or career. This may include procrastination or overworking to the point of chronic irritability or abusiveness. One of the most common expressions of Cain self-destructiveness, in modern industrial society, is the so-called Type A behavior. This is defined in medicine as

an action-emotion complex that can be observed in any person who is **aggressively** involved in a chronic, incessant struggle to achieve more and more in less and less time, and if required to do so, against the opposing efforts of other things or other persons.(13)

In its pure form Type A behavior heightens the possibility of a heart attack as early as age 35.

All of these symptoms reflect a personality being programmed largely out of the paroxysmal-epileptoid dimension. People who live and act out of this side are expected to make, as we all are, satisfying vocational choices. The decision socializes the inner needs and carries on the shared tasks of society. Throughout his long lifetime Szondi has carefully researched the patterns of choice in relation to the familial background. He has demonstrated that families are inclined to select certain kinds of vocations.

They who closely conform to the Cain profile generally move in two directions. On the one hand, they aim for the professions like the ministry, health care, legal services, social work, counseling, and the police. This pattern mirrors the well-known fact that often ministers and psychologists are also vulnerable to divorce, alcoholism, or suicide. It even fits a prominent line of research in sociology which notes profound similarities between police and criminals. Hans Toch has confirmed that law enforcement contains many violent men. "They reflect the same fears and insecurities, the same fragile, self-centered perspectives. They display the same bluster and bluff, panic and punitiveness, rancor and revenge ...."(14) These characteristics all belong to the Cain profile.

On the other hand, Cain types like rugged outdoor professions. In what has the appearance of a poetic theme, but is a significant psychiatric conclusion, Szondi has shown how the classical Greek elements-- air, earth, fire, and water--can function as Cain masks.(15) Going to sea in ships or joining the Air Force are socially respectable outlets for paroxysmal people. So is fire fighting. For even fire itself is as volatile, ambiguous, and fascinating as Cain himself. In modern society the terror of the arsonist and the heroism of fire men have become commonplace Cain opposites in many American cities.

26

Similarly, they who work on or beneath the earth are often highly paroxysmal. Whenever the farmers in the Midwest become disturbed over government policy, they mount their tractors and parade into Washington D. C. Nor can we easily forget that when the United Mine Workers go on strike, the towns and highways of coal mining states like Pennsylvania and West Virginia become dangerous. Historically, the American coal miner has been susceptible to ferocious Cain outbursts.

In light of these destinies, we should not put the Cain and Abel symbols into an urban-rural dichotomy. The homocidal potential lies everywhere. It is fashionable among some contemporary students of theology to make the family and nature as ideal models of an ultimate presence. The family seems to be a place of intimacy, and nature appears to be serene. But the family and nature can be just as lethal as the city. Murder is a primitive potential whenever two people disagree emotionally.

Genesis chapter four seems to symbolize the homocidal intent as all-pervasive. For in the genealogy Enoch is followed by Irad, Mehujael, Methushael, and Lamech. The latter occupies the seventh generation of Adam's family. Lamech marries Adah and Zillah, who bear him three sons.

Adah bore Jabal; he was the father of those who dwell in tents and have cattle. His brother's name was Jubal; he was the father of all those who play the lyre and pipe. Zillah bore Tubal-cain; he was the forger of all instruments of bronze and iron. (Gen. 4:20-22)

In Hebrew tradition the Kenites claim to be the descendants of Cain. Like their ancestor, they were all builders of cities. (I. Sam. 30:29) References to the Kenites appear infrequently, so not much is known about them. But in view of the symbolic character of the fourth chapter, we may use this term to designate the paroxysmal nature of all peoples. So in building cities, working as smiths, cattlemen, and artisans, Cain's descendants are all socializing their familial tendencies in civilization. Since their gene pool seems to be narrow, with much intermarriage, the likelihood of bringing latent patterns into dominance is high. Could we not speculate that the early biblical families are manifestly paroxysmal? Are they not uniquely susceptible to evil and its atonement?

Despite the obscurity of the historical references, we can at least use the Cain complex as a general theological formula. Theologians have for centuries seen the early chapters of Genesis as a narration of the origin of sin in the world. The Cain concept can also fulfill this role. For whenever we feel rage, hatred, envy, anger, jealousy, or vengeance, we are caught in the Cain predicament, pleading for an ultimate acceptance and lashing out against our brother. The formula fits our family life, and it also accounts for mass hostility such as fratricide and genocide. By analogy, historical fratricide symbolizes a quest for an immortality.

Whether individual or collective, the Cain formula identifies the concrete conditions of the estrangement of existence. Feeling the Cain passions is the same as being enslaved—from others and from our own freedom. Overcoming the Cain complex restores wholeness and integrity. This means that only we who resolve the Cain complex are entitled to call ourselves free and in control of our destinies. The only alternative to an unresolved Cain complex is a life of sin and evil.

The tragedy of a Cain life is that it makes us defenseless and vulnerable to accidents. One legend tells that Lamech was a blind hunter.(16) He would go hunting with the help of his son. The boy would find the game and position his father to shoot. One day they went hunting, and Lamech shot and killed a distant object. As they approached the fallen corpse, the son saw that it was a man with a horn on his forehead. He told Lamech that he had killed not an animal but a man. The father was seized with fear and guilt; for he had killed his ancestor Cain and broken the sign. Henceforth, to express his own homocidal fate he would kill with more and more cruelty.

This simple story illustrates that in the limited human gene pool the tendency to evil increases. Once we kill another person, our life is no longer free but in the grip of an enslaving and fateful force of emotion.

Footnotes

1. Albert Heim quoted in Russell Noyes and Roy Kletti, "Depersonalization in the Face of Life-Threatening Danger," **Psychiatry**, 39:1 (Feb., 1976), p. 19.

2. Gerhard von Rad, **Genesis**, trans. by J. Marks (Philadelphia: Westminster, 1961), p. 88.

3. Ibid., p. 93.

4. Carl Sagan, **The Dragons of Eden** (New York: Ballantine, 1978), pp. 96-97.

5. Helm Stierlin, "Hitler as the Bound Delegate of His Mother," **History of Childhood Quarterly**, 3:4 (Spring, 1976), pp. 471-473.

6. L. Szondi, **Schicksalsanalytische Therapie** (Bern: Hans Huber, 1963), p. 358.

7. Martin Buber, **Good and Evil**, trans. by M. Bullock (New York: Charles Scribner's Sons, 1952), p. 85.

8. "Cain," **The Jewish Encyclopedia**, III, p. 493.

9. L. Szondi, **Kain, Gestalten des Bösen** (Bern: Hans Huber, 1969), pp. 53-54.

10. Rollo May, **Power and Innocence** (New York: Norton, 1972), pp. 27-28.

11. Jacques Ellul, **The Meaning of the City**, trans. by D. Pardee (Grand Rapids: Eerdmans, 1970), p. 8.

12. Szondi, **Kain**, pp. 116-117.

13. Meyer Friedman and Ray Rosenman, **Type A Behavior and Your Heart** (New York: Alfred Knopf, 1974), p. 67.

14. Hans Toch, **Violent Men** (Chicago: Aldine, 1969), p. 240.

15. Szondi, **Kain**, pp. 78, 147-151.

16. Ibid., pp. 39-40.

Chapter Three: THE HEROIC ATONEMENT OF EVIL

I. The Destiny of Moses

The opening chapters of Genesis are symbolic accounts of the origins of human existence. The names of Cain and Abel, Adam and Eve, and others of their lineage may be used as models for reflection upon moral experience at any time and place. Although much of the Bible is a record of historical events, beginning with the call of Abraham in Genesis chapter twelve, nevertheless other names may also be taken as symbols. This is true for Moses who, though a prominent historical figure, has become an enduring symbol of a specific kind of destiny.

In the Hebrew-Christian tradition Moses is the pre-eminent ancient who has resolved the Cain complex. By virtue of his personal achievement he may be called heroic. For classical scholars the hero is the great man who has been summoned by a deity for a hazardous journey, who goes forth and confronts the forces of death and evil, and who finally returns to regenerate his society.(1) Moses' experience conforms to this heroic cycle. But what is unique in his case is that he undergoes the Cain event, overcomes its effects, and achieves a permanent principle of restitution.

Moses' resolution of the Cain complex can be demonstrated briefly by examining his biography. An appropriate organization of his life in five stages has been set forth by Szondi:(2)

A. **Prince.** Moses was born in Egypt during the fifteenth or sixteenth centuries B. C. E. The Hebrews had been living in Egypt for some time and had grown in number. The Pharoah feared that if his enemies the Hyksos were to attack, the Hebrews would take the opportunity to leave the country. So the King tried to limit the Hebrew population by decreeing that all male babies should be thrown into the Nile River.

In the tribe of Levi a woman conceived and bore a son. According to later tradition, her name was Jochebed and she was a Kenite. (Jg. 1:16, 4:11) During the first three months after her delivery, she hid the baby. Unable to conceal him any longer, she laid him in a basket made of bulrushes, setting it out among the reeds at the edge of the river.

Sometime later Pharoah's daughter came to the Nile to bathe. Hearing a baby crying, she looked around and saw the small basket in the reeds. She found the baby and, seeing he was Hebrew, decided to raise him because he was so beautiful. She arranged that he be nursed by another woman in her father's court. Eventually, he matured and became the son of Pharoah's daughter. She named him Moses.

But Moses' life in the royal household came to an end one day in his youth. He once saw an Egyptian beating a Hebrew. "He looked this way and that, and seeing no one he killed the Egyptian and hid him in the sand." (Ex. 2:12) Despite his Egyptian upbringing, apparently the sight of the beating was so traumatic that it re-awakened his ancestral identity. In response to his first crisis he drew upon his Hebrew heritage.

On the next day Moses intervened in a skirmish between two Hebrews. They wondered how he, a member of the royal house, could morally judge them. Did he intend to kill them as he had murdered the Egyptian? When Moses heard them say this, he became "afraid, and thought, 'Surely the thing is known.' When Pharoah heard of it, he sought to kill Moses." (Ex. 2:14b-15a) Once again in his young life Moses was haunted by a threat of death.

B. Shepherd. Suddenly possessed by fear, Moses fled from Egypt and headed into the wilderness. For some unanswered reason--to which we should return--Moses went toward the southern region of the Sinai, where the Midianites dwelled. Arriving there, he quickly won the friendship of Jethro, the Priest of Midian, for protecting his daughters from hostile shepherds. Jethro was pleased with Moses and invited his guest to become a member of his household. Moses accepted and became a shepherd. Later he married Zippora, Jethro's daughter.

While Moses tended sheep in the land of the Midianites, the King of Egypt died. He was succeeded by a more ruthless Pharoah. The working conditions of the Hebrews worsened. The Bible describes how they cried out for deliverance, and God heard their pleas. So God sought a man to lead the Hebrews out of Egyptian bondage. He would choose the shepherd Moses. The dramatic moment came one day, as Moses watched over his flock near Mt. Sinai.

"And the angel of the Lord appeared to him in a flame of fire out of the midst of the bush; and he looked, and lo, the bush was burning, yet it was not consumed." (Ex. 3:2) Speaking out of the fire, God declared that Moses was standing on holy ground. He should remove his shoes and stand in awe. For the voice announced that he was the God of Moses' father, of Abraham, Isaac, and Jacob.

In this fiery encounter Moses had a shock of recognition. The moment was a crisis that Moses was indeed a Hebrew and that the God of the burning bush was the Lord of his people. With the trauma of this discovery Moses became even more afraid and hid his face. While still trembling, he learned that his people remained oppressed in Egypt and that he would lead them out of bondage. After liberating the people, Moses would bring them back to this holy mountain and serve God anew.

Alarmed by this crisis, Moses protested. He said he could not be a leader, and he had no power. But God promised to be with him and give him sufficient power. Finally in a dramatic plea, Moses stammered: "Oh, my Lord, I am not eloquent, either heretofore or since thou hast spoken to thy servant; but I am slow of speech and of tongue." (Ex. 4:10) Moses confessed that he was a stutterer. This only provoked ferocious anger from God.

C. **Miracle-Worker.** God assigns Aaron the Levite to be Moses' spokesman. The latter also received a staff to perform miraculous signs. Both returned to Egypt, confronted the King, and demanded he release the Hebrews. Pharoah refused their request and admitted that he did not know God. God then retaliated by hardening Pharoah's heart and producing signs and wonders. Through Aaron and Moses he released the plagues of serpents, floods, frogs, gnats, flies, cattle, boils, hail, locusts, and darkness.

But the King remained undaunted until that night when God displayed his cruelty.

At midnight the Lord smote all the first-born in the land of Egypt, from the first-born of Pharoah who sat on his throne to the first-born of the captive who was in the dungeon, and all the first-born of the cattle. (Ex. 12:29)

33

Amid the anguished cries of the night, Moses led his people out of Egypt. They journeyed by a pillar of cloud at day and a pillar of fire at night. Crossing the Red Sea, they proceeded south toward Mt. Sinai. On the way they fought the Amelekites and finally arrived at the holy mountain. Moses returned to his family after the long ordeal. Jethro praised what God had done for the people and offered a sacrifice in his name.

D. **Leader of the People.** Once again Moses ascended Sinai and beheld God in a vision. God announced a Covenant between himself and his people. The form of the Sinai Covenant conforms to the suzerainty type of treaty developed by the ancient Hittites. Such a treaty had six elements which, in comparison with the Sinai version, has the following outline:(3)

1. **Prologue.** The Covenant opens with an affirmation of divine sovereignty: "I am the Lord your God ...." (Ex. 20:2a)

2. **Historical Survey.** It restates what God has accomplished: "brought you out of the land of Egypt ...." (Ex. 20:2b)

3. **Oath and Stipulations.** The oath binds the stronger party, God, to the weaker human party. Psychologically, we could interpret the Covenant as a fulfillment of the law of participation. Sharing in the Covenant guarantees transcendence and identity for the people. The stipulations of the Covenantal participation comprise the Ten Commandments. (Ex. 20:13-17) These principles actually prescribe restitution for the Cain event and its equivalents.

(a.) "You shall have no other gods before me." The transcendent God is affirmed and alien deities or projections are dismissed.

(b.) "You shall not make yourself a graven image ...." Similarly, God cannot be represented in simple subject-object forms. By rejecting all objectifiable concepts, the Law relativizes the world of space, time and projections, and reveals God as an abstract horizon.

(c.) "You shall not take the name of the Lord your God in vain ...." Since in biblical religion a name manifests the essence of a person, uttering God's name makes a false claim to an ultimate power. Saying the divine name inflates the self beyond its normal limits.

(d.) "Remember the Sabbath ...." Instead we ought to re-enact the seventh day of Creation, on which God rested, as an ethical framework for our experience.

(e.) "Honor your father and your mother ...." The family of origin conditions one's basic needs and tendencies. Thus, respect for parents is a repayment for what one has received.

(f.) You shall not murder, commit adultery, steal, or covet a neighbor's house. The next four commands prohibit various forms of the Cain event. The Law stipulates that these lethal manifestations be controlled so as to protect the Covenant community.

(g.) "You shall not bear false witness ...." Lying is an unreliable defense against the Cain impulses. Like denial or repression lying is simply a way to change the meaning of a social field in order to escape threatening circumstances.

4. **Deposit of Rules and Proclamation.** The Covenant is put in the ark and placed in the Most Holy Place. (Ex. 25:16) This is preceded by Moses' public announcement of the treaty. Public proclamation is a means of visible validation for the oral memory. Inscribing the commands on the tablets serves as guidelines for the retention of the treaty in the oral tradition.

5. **Witnesses.** Since the treaty prohibits other deities, no witnesses are present--except the people themselves. (Josh. 24:21-22)

6. **Curses and Blessings.** Keeping the statutes brings blessings to the people; breaking them, curses. (Deut. 27:15-29:1; Lev. 17-26) This command connects the Law with the act-fate structure of moral experience.

E. **Politician and Despot.** The Sinai treaty establishes the Hebrews as the People of God in a political form. The Covenant and the ordinances together constitute the Law as a transcendent prin-

35

ciple of holiness, justice, and goodness. But the Law
also exercises a psychological function. It provides
an objective framework by which the Cain emotions may
be socialized and controlled. The Law guarantees the
restitution of evil and a means of freedom for those
who resolve the Cain complex.

The structure of atonement does not eliminate the
homocidal intent. Rather the Cain emotions are projected onto the Kingdom of God and maintained with
considerable irony and cruelty. The following passage
illustrates this point:

> ... then Moses stood in the gate of the
> camp, and said, "Who is on the Lord's side?
> Come to me." And all the sons of Levi
> gathered themselves together to him. And he
> said to them. "Thus says the Lord God of
> Israel, 'Put every man his sword on his
> side, and go to and fro from gate to gate
> throughout the camp, and slay every man his
> brother, and every man his companion, and
> every man his neighbor.'" (Ex. 32:26-27)

They who deviate from the Law are destroyed. (Nb.
25:5) As in Rabbinic theology, Moses serves God with
the evil drive. Having begun his destiny by murdering
an Egyptian, Moses reaches a climax by slaying thou-
sands of his people. It therefore seems fitting that
when the Hebrews finally arrive at the edge of the
Promised Land, God speaks to Moses: "I will give it
to your descendants. I have let you see it with your
eyes, but you shall not go over there." (Deut. 34:4b)
So Moses perishes as he has lived--in the grip of the
divine passion.

II. The Psychology of Moses' Heroism

Moses' savage character prompts us to ask why he
was what he was. While his personality is historically inaccessible to us, the well-known Kenite
hypothesis may permit us to offer a speculative
interpretation. Though conjectural, a psychological
portrait of Moses can at least yield insight into his
destiny. The clue to a reconstruction lies in the
fact that the Judges tradition identifies Moses'
mother as a Kenite. Jochebed married Amram, a Levite.
(Ex. 6:20)

The Kenites were a Semitic tribe who claimed to descend from Cain. They were friendly with the Hebrews and intermarried with them, even during the Egyptian period.(4) Since Cain was a paroxysmal-epileptoid personality, this permits us to infer that such a set of tendencies might have been transmitted by Kenite descent. In view of the fact that the Hebrew and Kenite tribes comprised a narrow gene pool, could we not further infer that Cain-like paroxysmality was transmitted in the families of Israel? Certainly, the explosive behavior of the prophets and kings of Israel could be called paroxysmal. Moses was clearly paroxysmal, and he must have inherited this disposition from his Kenite mother.

By making this assumption, we are able to answer further questions. Why in facing his first crisis does Moses turn to murder? Why, after committing the crime, does he flee to the Midianites? Why not south toward Luxor, or north to the sea? It is surely no accident that he joined the Midianites. For historically they were related to the Kenites.(5) So Jethro and his daughters were actually his relatives. And marrying Zippora illustrates how we often choose our marriage partners in terms of familial influences.

It is also not surprising that Moses chooses to become a shepherd in the desert. Working out of doors among the elements is a useful way to socialize a vibrant emotional disposition. But Moses was soon to acquire a new destiny, which demanded of him a more radical vocational choice. The way he became the great and heroic leader, while in the desert, contains three crucial characteristics.(6) By putting these three together we can establish a meaningful profile of the Hebrew prophet.

A. The Murderer. When God elects a prophet, he adopts a murderer. Why should he even consider a man who has slain a brother? Why not pick an innocent man? The selection of a murderer as a prophet is not unusual in biblical religion, as the biography of the apostle Paul implies. The prophet who has taken life in passion now, by the grace of God, saves life in the same passion. It seems that the prophetic call presupposes the logic of the Cain complex as the context of revelation.

Choosing a murderer, further, establishes a connection between revelation and Creation. In as much as the roots of murder lie in the archaic depths of nature, then these need to be atoned for in the redemption of evil. Unless the prophet experiences the root of evil, he cannot become an exemplary and compelling witness to the atonement. The revelation would lack a realistic basis.

B. **The Visionary.** What is significant is that Moses' vocational choice occurs in a genuine theophany. The prophet encounters God with fear, trembling, and ecstasy. This suggests that primitive emotion is the vehicle of revelation. Since murder and ecstasy grow out of emotion, then they both have the same location in human nature--the old mammalian stratum of the brain. Were Moses an intellectual or a depressive, his receptivity of the revelation would be blocked. For only a surcharged emotional state can bypass cerebral controls and make one susceptible to a transcendent encounter.

C. **The Stutterer.** It is not unusual in the history of religion to find sickness among the heroic figures. Faith is not immune to pathology. We have come to realize, after the contributions of modern psychiatry, that no one is purely healthy. In fact, many of the important medical advances since the second world war have shown the relationship between physical illness and emotional disturbances.

It is common in psychiatry to speak of psychic equivalents. This is because humans inherit genetically a reaction range to specific crises and environmental hazards. Our familial background gives us a set of lethal possibilities which vary as life ebbs and flows. In families dominated by paroxysmal-epileptoid patterns, we can construct a continuum of disorders. At one end we could put the pure Cain event and, at the other end, an equally hard-core medical equivalent: the triad of epilepsy, migraines, and stuttering. In between lie the psychosomatic ailments as discussed in the preceding chapter. All of these disorders are symptoms of massive emotional upheavals taking place in the subcortical regions of the brain.

Moses was therefore a murderer, a visionary, and a stutterer. Each of these conditions is a mask of the Cain complex as it moves toward resolution.

38

III. The Restitution of Goodness

Karl Barth has taught that the Creation has been accomplished and that its inner fulfillment is present in the Covenant.(7)   The Creation is the external structure of the Covenant.   The theological correlation of Creation and the Covenant lays the foundation for the ethical order of human experience.   Since the Covenant and the Law are extensions of Creation, they are valid at any time and place.

Szondian psychiatry makes a fundamental contribution to theological ethics in its theory of conscience.   The atonement of evil is the definition of conscience.   The profound insight of this notion is that it locates good, evil, and the reinstatement of the good within nature.   The relationship between these experiences is cyclical.   What is important is that the biological organism be viewed as a self-renewing moral system.

With this definition Szondi goes beyond the individualistic ideas of conscience.   Under the impact of psychoanalysis, we often interpret conscience as the internalization of what we ought not to do and be. The content of this introjection comes from what the father believes is normative.   In order to maintain conscience a portion of the aggression factor must be internalized in the moral content.   This sets up an Oedipal conflict between what we want to do and what the father thinks we ought to do.   The result is the inclination to resolve moral issues privatistically. Krister Stendahl has called this the "introspective conscience."(8)

The difficulty with an introspective definition is that it makes morality a problem of obedience. Either we obey or disobey an authority figure.   This dichotomistic understanding has been common in the Protestant tradition, and it has been influential in the interpretation of Genesis chapter three.   But as we have seen in our preceding discussions, Adam and Eve are not engaged in a disobedient rebellion from God.   They are initiating a new kind of experience that leads us toward the good, the evil, and restitution.

The Szondian model conforms accurately to Rabbinic usage.   Although the Hebrew Scriptures lack a rational theory of conscience, as found among the

Stoics, they point to a process of committing an evil, acknowledging guilt, judging that sin has occurred, and atoning for it. The Rabbinic equivalent of conscience is the examination of evil deeds.(9) Such an examination takes place with individuals and with communities. The social form of the Hebrew conscience is the Day of Atonement ritual. As prescribed by the Law of Moses, this liturgy cleanses the people and maintains the Creation.

Conscience is not reducible to cultural conditioning or individual introspection. It is an innate biological function and developed through socialization and conscious choice. By virtue of the Creation all people are endowed with the ability to perform evil and to atone for it. Since conscience conforms to the order of nature, it survives as a residual factor even when the forms of civilization are destroyed. In certain boundary-line conditions, such as the outbursts of radical evil in the twentieth century, the distinctions between good and evil do not pass away.

Thus, the capacity to live in accord with law does not depend upon the rise and fall of civilizations. The Mosaic vision of justice and goodness is a permanent legacy. The correlation of Creation and Law, to which the Bible witnesses, is the ultimate foundation for human destiny.

Footnotes

1. Joseph Campbell, The Hero With a Thousand Faces (New York: Pantheon, 1949), p. 30.

2. L. Szondi, Moses, Antwort auf Kain (Bern: Hans Huber, 1973), pp. 105-113.

3. Dewey Beegle, Moses, The Servant of Yahweh (Grand Rapids: Eerdmans, 1972), p. 204.

4. Roland de Vaux, The Early History of Israel, trans. by D. Smith (Philadelphia: Westminster, 1978), pp. 332-333.

5. H. H. Rowley, From Joseph to Joshua (London: Oxford, 1950), p. 169.

6. Szondi, Moses, p. 107.

7.   Karl Barth, Church Dogmatics, III/3, pp. 6-8.

8.   Krister Stendahl, Paul Among Jews and Gentiles (Philadelphia: Fortress, 1976), p. 78.

9.   H. Jaeger, "L'Examen de Conscience dans les Religions Non-Chretiennes et avant le Christianisme," Numen, 6 (1959), p. 209.

Chapter Four: RADICAL EVIL AND THE DEMONIC

I. Destiny and the Demonic

A theory of human destiny in the twentieth century cannot ignore the global iruptions of radical evil and claim any validity. The enormous destruction of life and civilization, the traumatic uprooting of millions from their homelands, and the sudden rise of savage tyrannies have become commonplace in modern history. The political spectacles have shown that genocide, one of the most advanced forms of evil, has become policy in some states. The foremost theological task, therefore, is to comprehend, if possible, the unprecedented scale of evil.

There are several approaches to the problem in current discussions. A dominant argument, espoused by social critics and theologians, is that radical evil is the product of advanced industrial society.(1) Advocates of this idea say that the destruction of populations requires a highly efficient technological system, capable of mass producing sophisticated weapons, centralizing vast political powers, and moving people and material over wide distances. This kind of organization grows out of the modern secularizing tendencies of civilization. The fact of such an organization at this time in history leads to the charge that the system is evil rather than the people who work within it.

This argument presupposes that the bureaucratic system is a rigid hierarchy. If we may define the state as society acting as a whole, then the function takes on a hierarchical form, specifically a vertical line of command-obedience relationships. A political hierarchy is efficient in the execution of evil because we, the members, occupy our respective niches. We receive orders from our superiors and discharge them to our subordinates.

The crucial issue is that the command-obedience circuit of authority erodes our moral responsibility.(2) We carry out orders by simple obedience, not fully responsible for the fact that the entire system commits great evil. This implies that the actual perpetrators of evil are ordinary citizens, like you and me, who are simply doing their jobs. The same point was made by Hannah Arendt during the war crimes trial of Adolf Eichmann in 1961. This man, who had overseen the Nazi concentration camps, had appeared a banal and pathetic civil servant to Arendt.(3)

While the exposure of political bureaucracy as a form of evil is correct, this line of thought fails to explain why functionaries are attracted to the system and how millions can be aroused to passionate assent. There must be profound motivations for people to fit into a totalistic system which runs by abstract regulations and mechanized efficiency. No state can last without the consent of its people, and when the participation becomes one of passion, then the issue is more than a rational assent. Just to say that an administrator of evil is banal does not penetrate to the depths of his attraction.

We must also recognize the role of the charismatic leader in the totalitarian state. Such a leader, who assumes power by a unique appeal and talent, reflects the same needs and conflicts of his supporters. He can "appeal to a defeated, resentful people ... of frustrated ambitions ... who are in search of a unifying belief system which would satisfy unfulfilled needs ... and ... make amends for the grievance of his people."(4)

An attraction occurs when two or more persons share the same hereditary needs and acquired conflicts, particularly those involving sexual disturbances, moral complaints, and interpersonal insecurity. What distinguishes the charismatic leader from his followers is that he has lived through the same dilemmas as they and gives the appearance of a personal integration. It is not that he is truly whole but that he creates the impression of having conquered the same problems.

The widespread attraction of the people to a leader electrifies the society. The people are exalted because they are able to transfer their unresolved needs onto the leader and experience a satisfaction. The social elation embodies a mystic element in the sense that the lonely and alienated person is brought into a broader bond. The leader exercises a parental care and sets up a pervasive attachment. It is easy to understand how the so-called obedience to authority works within the charism. The burden of the moral consciousness is lifted, and the individual projects the weight of responsibility onto the leader. He then assumes one's fears and guilts in a public display of care.

We can see this problem in large states and in small religious cults. Obeying the commands of the leader gives one an acquired stability. As long as we cannot perceive a connection with the external evil, then we can presume normality. But in fact the normal routine is really a mask. The elation may block moral insight and only heighten a repressed guilt. Such guilt, and consequent anxiety, can come from the fact that we have not fulfilled our own needs for moral development.

One of the reasons for the erosion of individual conscience is that in modern states specialized squads perform police, military, and terrorist functions. An aura surrounding secret societies has emerged, and it is identified in the use of initials to designate them, such as KGB, CIA, Savak, and so on. In the Nazi period the outstanding example was the SS, particularly its Order of the Death's Head, which directly supervised the concentration camps. Adolf Hitler created the SS in 1925 as a kind of Praetorian Guard. In 1929 Heinrich Himmler assumed command.

The SS was a popular group, consisting mainly of unemployed war veterans. But contrary to what we have heard, it was not an efficient hierarchy.(5) It was more like a cult, fanatically devoted to Hitler himself, committed to the use of brute force on behalf of his wishes and even prepared to murder one another if necessary, that is, if one were disloyal. Members were recruited out of Nordic stock, preferably those with blonde hair, blue eyes, and pure genealogies since 1750.

The SS elite was to be fearless and cruel and the vanguard of Nazi ideology. Its internal psychological organization corresponds to the Cain model: love of the father (Hitler) and hatred of the brother (other Germans). Many of the members were characterized by drive conflicts, such as sado-masochistic aggression (sexual), exhibitionist rage and hatred (paroxysmal), totalitarian ideology (ego), and dependency (contact). The remainder of the chapter will show how these conflicts were also present in Hitler himself.

While the Nazi elite bore the Cain passions, a full Cain complex was not present. The Cain experience was not carried through to its completion, to an Abel state, a moral restitution. In the place of a Cain-Moses or -Abel polarity, this historical era demonstrated, in Hitler and his associates, serious disintegration. The significance of this is that when the personality disintegrates, the hereditary needs split and become more dangerous. The purpose of studying the Hitler biography is to demonstate how disintegration or splitting is the source of radical evil in persons.

Accordingly, we will follow Szondi's theory of drive disintegration, because it is one of the most comprehensive available today. Unfortunately, contemporary theology has not kept up with psychiatry in the investigation of evil. But in the older literature there is an idea which may function as the theological equivalent of radical evil. It is the demonic. Originally proposed by Paul Tillich, the demonic may be defined as a movement, from the archaic depths of nature, of dreadful and fascinating terror, that destroys all form and reduces life to chaos.(6)

Generally, Tillich used the demonic to characterize political movements. But it could also refer to individual experiences of possession with the passion to destroy. The idea of the demonic is implied in the Cain story, precisely at the point when the eldest son of Adam feels the force of the temptation to slay his brother. But the demonic as such goes beyond the Cain cycle in a crucial way. The demonic is destruction for its own sake, thus lacking restitution. Since the demonic breaks the cycle of atonement, it may be called anti-divine.

This notion fits those modern societies which act as a whole to achieve pure, non-redemptive evil. This manifests the function of a totalitarian state. But the demonic is also at work in religious cults, where the leaders claim to be divine and to establish a perfect society on earth. The latter takes shape around the charismatic leaders who attract their followers into mystic bonds, full of elation and intrigue. For despite the complex order of technology, evil still functions as a temptation. And it is precisely through our capacity to feel ecstasy that we may be lead into temptation.

In times of great danger the lure of political transcendence is exhilarating. The passion to be free

46

of the burdensome conscience can drive us into the
arms of a charismatic leader, whose external charms
conceal his hidden psychopathology. The promise of
his ecstasy is to alleviate us of the weight of
decision-making. Choosing our destinies has become
increasingly difficult in mass, bureaucratic societies. Often it is easier to let a public figure
choose for us.

But the conversion of choice into obedience sets
up a fateful process for the lonely individual. It is
due to the nature of evil and its violent ecstasy that
we should not make freedom the central category in a
theology. Since freedom converts into its opposite,
into fate, a concept is necessary to account for the
polarity. Such a notion is that of destiny, an idea
as old and as rich as that of the demonic.

The remainder of this chapter examines the fate
of a charismatic political leader in the early decades
of the twentieth century. The figure chosen is Adolf
Hitler; for he illustrates an eminent person who was
capable of widespread attraction and yet whose life
was driven tragically by a deep-seated disintegration.

II. Adolf Hitler: A Paroxysmal-Paranoid

So many books and articles have been written
about this strange and repelling figure. But none
have approached his life in terms of the psychology of
destiny. In consultation with Szondi, I propose that
Hitler be seen as an example of a paroxysmal-
paranoid.(7)

A. **Ancestry.** Since a personal destiny is
influenced by the family background, we should examine
the Hitler genealogy and point out the critical
patterns. Hitler's begins with Anna Maria Schicklgruber who gave birth to an illegitimate son named
Alois on June 7, 1937 in Döllersheim, Austria. She
was 41 years old when she bore the future father of
Adolf Hitler.

Maria never identified her lover. In 1930 a
relative of Adolf Hitler, in an attempted blackmail,
said the father of Alois was a Jew named Franken-
berger. He was allegedly a wealthy householder, for
whom Maria worked as a maid. Subsequent research on
this controversy has failed to prove the identity of
the man. But at least Adolf Hitler feared he might

have had a Jewish grandfather and therefore tried to hide his ancestry throughout his life.(8)

In 1842 Maria married Johann Georg Hiedler, a wandering mill worker. Young Alois was not liked by Hiedler, so the boy had to be raised by the elder Hiedler's brother, Johann Nepomuk. But when Maria died in 1847, Alois was left at the mercy of his stepfather. As we might expect, at the age of thirteen Alois left home and fled to Vienna. Later, Adolf Hitler would approvingly describe Alois who "laced his tiny knapsack and ran away from home" as desperate and adventurous.(9)

By age nineteen, Alois had secured a job with the Imperial Board of Revenue. After doing this for nine years, he changed to that of a customs officer. While he publically displayed initiative and efficiency, privately he was sexually aggressive and promiscuous. He fathered a child out of wedlock and then married the wealthy Anna Glasl, a woman fourteen years older than he.

Anna's money enabled Alois to secure Klara Pölzl as a maid. All three lived together in the Braunau inn. Alois became sexually involved with Fanni Matzelsberger, one of the employees in the kitchen of the inn. Angered at Alois' liaison, Anna divorced him in 1880. Alois then married Fanni who, though ill with tuberculosis, lived with him until her death in 1884. During this period, Klara left the household for work elsewhere.

However, before marrying Fanni, Alois illegally changed his name from Schicklgruber to Hitler, a variation of Hiedler. In 1876 Johann Nepomuk Hiedler, with three witnesses, told the parish priest at Döllersheim that his brother was actually Alois' father. This may well have been true, but Johann Georg had been dead for twenty years and could not verify the claim. But the priest improperly accepted the testimony and entered the Hiedler patrimony into the register. While the motive was not clear, the name change gave Alois a new respectability.

After Fanni died, Alois renewed his sexual interest in Klara. He coaxed her back and proposed marriage. But with the name change, Alois' father and Klara's grandfather turned out to be brothers; so the prospective marriage would be consanguineous. Alois needed a Papal dispensation from Rome. It was granted, and they were married on January 7, 1885. Alois was 48, Klara 25.

The family into which Alois married had a history of mental and physical disorders. An affidavit in the Linz archives identifies Johanna, Klara's irascible sister, as a probable schizophrenic.(10) Klara's nephew, the son of her other sister Theresia, was a hunchback with a speech defect. Klara was perceived as a quiet, sad, and disappointed woman, who was also suspicious and afraid. She looked upon her husband as an awesome figure and addressed him as uncle.

Alois was seen as "a restless individual, always taking something up and then dropping it again."(11) He would move his family from town to town for no apparent reason. His salary was substantial, and he was frugal. Alois' friends perceived him as strict, strong-willed, and capable of great anger. But they did not regard him as a drunkard. Emanuel Lugert, a friend of Alois, testified that he drank only moderately, stopping by the inn in the afternoon for a "couple of pints--seldom more than three.... But he had a good head. I never saw him tight, and he always started back home in good time for supper."(12)

In this culture incest and illegitimacy were common. Where these are prevalent, it is quite likely that latent recessive genes tend to become manifest. One out of three of us carries a gene for a mental defect. Of the three Pölzl sisters, Theresia is the carrier of a physical deformity. In as much as Johanna is a probable schizophrenic, this is highly significant for the family. Schizophrenia is inherited recessively. This means that the Pölzl parents are both carriers. Therefore, it is quite probable that Klara carries a latent schizophrenia.

With respect to Alois' family, it is more difficult to make a genetic analysis. Since his paternity has never been proven decisively, it remains impossible to do so. However, the conclusions of Szondi's research permit us to make at least a judgment. His explosive emotional behavior, his nomadic life-style, his tendencies toward arrogance and exhibitionism, as in his desire to display himself proudly in uniform, all suggest a paroxysmal manner. At the same time his marriage choices betray a sexual aggressiveness in the sense of an ambivalence or

49

compulsion. His ego manifests a stern willfulness and his contact sphere shows a restless manic quality.

In marriage choices paroxysmal persons are often attracted to those of a schizoid temperament. Klara's condition was the kind generally ascribed to paranoia. The formula for this is quite succinct: projection without participation equals paranoia. This means that when ego projections do not create relationships in ordinary experience, but are ends in themselves, a paranoic condition obtains.

Putting Klara's paranoia and Alois' paroxysmality together, we can understand the fundamental familial possibilities that Adolf Hitler inherits when he is born on April 20, 1889.

B. Childhood. Adolf Hitler was not the only child in the family. Alois had fathered Alois Jr. illegitimately and Angela legitimately. Fanni cared for them as long as she was alive. Klara assumed their care when she married Alois. She conceived and gave birth to three children who died: Gustav (1885-1887), Ida (1886-1888), and Otto (1887-1887).

Klara claimed that Adolf was a pale and sickly child. But a maid has remembered him as a "very healthy, lively child who developed very well."[13] As I look at Hitler's baby picture, I agree with the maid. This implies that Klara probably projected an image of weakness onto her baby, because of her anxiety at losing three others. The succession of deaths was no doubt a crisis that drew out the projective schizoform tendencies in her hereditary background.

Hitler's infancy has been of great interest to psychoanalysts. Rudolph Binion has written an influential paper proving that Klara breast fed Adolf for about two years, an allegedly long time of over-indulgence. He argues that the extended feeding is the psychological source of Hitler's later foreign policy of aggressively achieving more feeding ground for the German people in Eastern Europe.[14] This presupposes the doctrine--of learning theory and psychoanalysis--that the need for nourishment is primary and the source of all attachments.

Binion's argument is misleading because it identifies the parent-child relation as the origin of aggression. In contrast, it is necessary to distinguish, as demonstrated in ethology, between the sexual and contact drives. The mother is indeed the primal object of the infant's seeking and bonding. The contact needs are satisfied primarily through care and security rather than being fed. Feeding is secondary to the profound need for acceptance. The lack of security can then trigger aggressiveness and repress tenderness.

The problem with Klara's extended breast feeding is that she apparently could not distinguish between Adolf's cries for hunger and his cries for acceptance. It is not the extended breast feeding that is so bad; it is rather the erroneous assumption that feeding alone creates security. Consequently, it appears that Hitler's infancy was a time of anxiety and insecurity, a period of unsatisfied contact needs. Clinically, this can develop into frustration-aggression.

The psychoanalysts are more accurate, however, when they identify a sexual trauma during Adolf's third year of life.(15) There is a passage in **Mein Kampf**, where Hitler imagines a worker's family, consisting of seven, living in a small apartment. The parent-child relationships are tumultuous. Hitler infers

the character they will inevitably assume if this mutual quarrel takes the form of brutal attacks of the father against the mother, of drunken beatings, is hard for anyone who does not know this milieu to imagine.(16)

At the end of the passage he shifts to the first person, thus suggesting the situation was in his own family. Since there were no other families he could have observed, this one is probably his own.

The father's attacks, so characteristic of paroxysmal types, could have been beatings, rapes, or both. Either kind functions as a trauma for a child, particularly if one sees the parents in coitus. Clinically, the sexual assault, which psychoanalysis calls the primal scene, is introjected, and it imprints a view of sexuality as brutal and dangerous. Psychoanalysis has demonstrated that a beating or a sexual trauma is one origin of sado-masochistic perversions in the adult.(17) This conforms to

51

Szondi's research in which sexuality, through its aggressive component, is easily influenced by the early childhood environment.(18)

The critical phase of emotional disturbances is partly the first three years, as it is with sexuality, but also with the childhood ages of six to eight. Alois Jr. has given us a clear report on the critical Cain phase in Adolf's childhood.

He was imperious and quick to anger from childhood onward and would not listen to anyone. My step-mother always took his part. He would get the craziest notions and get away with it. If he didn't have his way, he got very angry .... He had no friends, took to no one and could be very heartless. He could fly into a rage over any triviality.(19)

This excessive, lonely rage seems to be an example of a paroxysmal alienation, which is one form of ego splitting.(20) With this report we can imagine the young Hitler projecting blame for any fault onto others, failing to relate well to the environment, and living in terms of a near total fantasy system. His childhood fantasy was so well developed that his first vocational choice was that of a priest. He was enthralled with the liturgical splendor of the Roman Catholic Church and he identified in his imagination with it.

Otherwise, his childhood was fairly normal. He attended elementary school and received good grades. He played cowboy and Indian games and liked to dominate the other children by talking loudly. Much of his childhood was also devoted to reading Karl May's novels about the American West, a practice he continued into adulthood.

Meanwhile Alois Jr. had run away from home in a desire to escape the oppressive control of his father. Adolf's younger brother Edmund had been born in 1894 and probably triggered a Cain rivalry.(21) But Edmund died of measles at age six. Since Adolf was eleven, it is likely that Edmund's death heightened his narcissistic quality and led him to regard himself as a unique survivor. Outlasting the other children, with whom he had expressed Cain emotions, could easily contribute to a paroxysmal-paranoia.

C. **Adolescence.** The crucial event that seems to begin Adolf's teen-age years was the death of Alois on January 3, 1903. The outstanding fact about the death is that Adolf does not carry on a normal grieving pattern. The failure to grieve presupposes the absence of a strong parental bond.

As an adolescent, Adolf was perceived by a teacher as follows:

> I can recall the gaunt, pale-faced youth pretty well. He had definite talent, though in a narrow field. But he lacked self-discipline, being notoriously cantankerous, wilful, arrogant, and irascible.(22)

These characteristics also came out of the paroxysmal-paranoid sources. But the friends of Adolf testify that these traits were enhanced after the death of Alois. Klara said: "He's as pig-headed as his father;" and Josef Mayrhofer admitted: "A stubborn fellow, like his father, the old Hitler."(23)

August Kubizeck, Adolf's teen-age friend, thought that Alois' restless, nomadic behavior was also in his son. Kubizeck felt that Adolf looked like Klara, particularly in the eyes: "They were the light eyes of his mother, but her somewhat staring, penetrating gaze was even more marked in the son and had even more force and expressiveness."(24)

Statements like these have led psychohistorians to see an Oedipus complex in Hitler. The formula of this complex is as follows: the son loves the mother and hates the father. On the surface, this idea may have some cogency. Alois' harsh, domineering attitude toward Adolf and the solicitous overindulgent behavior of Klara may have induced an Oedipal pattern.

Concerning the Oedipus complex, there is a compelling argument in Szondi's writings. He argues that this complex exists only when the mother sees her own father manifest in the son.(25) By her own testimony, Klara saw Alois not Johann Pölzl in Adolf's behavior. The Oedipal argument is further weakened by the fact that Adolf acts without deep emotional bonds with either parent. He does not so much love Klara as look like her.

Certainly, there is no fully developed Cain complex in Hitler either--because he does not make amends for his paroxysmality. While there are occasional Oedipal conflicts, it appears that the following formula best fits the young Hitler: When he acts paranoically, he is taking after his mother. When he behaves like a Cain type, he is taking after his father. Neither the Cain nor the Oedipus complex is fully present.

In the summer of 1905 Adolf developed a lung infection, and on the advice of a physician dropped out of school in the fall. Respiratory illnesses had been in the family. Leaving school allowed him to become a drifter, which was also a family tendency. Now Adolf Hitler could devote his time to pursue his ambition of becoming an artist. Together with his friend Kubizeck he would practice piano playing, draw architectural sketches, and attend Wagnerian operas.

A dramatic incident took place in October, 1906. He and Kubizeck attended a performance of Wagner's **Rienzi**. Hitler was so deeply moved by the tragic hero Rienzi that he identified with him and left the theatre in a trance. In a state of possession, he spoke of a special mission he would one day receive. Kubizeck listened

> with astonishment and emotion to what burst forth from him with elementary force. I will not attempt to interpret this phenomenon, but it was a state of complete ecstasy and rapture, in which he transferred the character of **Rienzi**, without even mentioning him as a model or example, with visionary power to the plane of his own ambitions.(26)

The ecstasy occurs in the ego state of inflation, a mechanism common among dreamy adolescents.

By the beginning of 1907, Hitler felt that he had become too harassed for his artistic plans by his brother-in-law Leo Raubal. Leo wanted Adolf to get a job. But Adolf hated Leo and thought he was nothing more than a dull civil servant. Being highly narcissistic, Adolf believed he was superior, so he decided to visit Vienna to fulfill his artistic destiny.

In September, 1907, Adolf took the entrance exam at the Vienna Academy of Art, in the school of painting. Hitler passed the composition test but failed the drawing test and was rejected. He was shocked by the failure and lashed out with great rage at the school. Lacking any self-insight as to why he was rejected, he preferred to project the blame onto the teachers. But meanwhile he concealed the test score from his family and maintained the appearance of being a student. He became simply a tourist.

However, in a few weeks Adolf was called home. Klara was dying of breast cancer. During the previous January a malignant breast had been removed by Dr. Karl Urban. The cancer spread so much that Dr. Edward Bloch, the family physician, applied painful iodoform treatments. These too failed to halt the disease.

Historians have debated when exactly Adolf returned home. Did he arrive in November to care for his dying mother? Or did he come after her death merely to collect the inheritance? While this issue is a matter of dispute, Klara did die on December 21, 1907. Her death seemed to be a crucial trauma for Hitler, so much so that on this Christmas and on subsequent holidays he would plunge into a deep depression. Yet the friends of Hitler do not confirm a normal grieving process in the following months.

Instead, according to Kubizeck, Hitler's rage and resentment boiled over. In February, 1908 the two went to Vienna, Hitler to try to re-apply to the academy, Kubizeck to attend the conservatory. The latter noticed that Adolf "had become unbalanced. He would fly into a temper at the slightest thing."(27) This is an insight into an advancing disintegration of Adolf's paroxysmal nature, a condition brought on by an abnormal grieving process for his mother.

III. Hitler's Demonic Fate

Hitler's second attempt to enter the Academy of Art also failed. Perhaps out of shame, he concealed this fact from everyone and abandoned Kubizeck in the fall of 1908. He virtually disappeared into the depths of the city, living as a tramp and trying to survive by selling inexpensive paintings. By 1909 he came of legal age and should have registered for the draft. He escaped the authorities successfully until 1914 when he showed up in Munich.

A. **Vocational Choice.** Ironically, when the first world war broke out, he enthusiastically joined the German army. A war hysteria swept the country and Hitler was caught up in it. He served with distinction in the army but did not advance beyond the rank of corporal. The war provided an opportune crisis to draw out quite clearly his own hereditary tendencies. The following letter, written from the front to a friend, indicates an emerging paranoic perception of politics.

> ... that those of us who are lucky enough to return to the fatherland will find it a purer place, less riddled with foreign influences, so that the daily sacrifices ... and the torrent of blood that keeps flowing ... against an international world of enemies, will not only help to smash Germany's foes outside but that our inner internationalism, too, will collapse.(28)

Hitler was in combat until blinded by a mustard gas attack in October, 1918. He entered Pasewalk hospital to recuperate. But in November, after learning of the armistice, he suffered a relapse in an apparently hysterical blindness. He explains:

> ... I could stand it no longer. It became impossible for me to sit still one minute more. Again everything went black before my eyes; I tottered and groped my way back to the dormitory, threw myself on my bunk, and dug my burning head into my blanket and pillow. (29)

He goes on to say, concerning the next few nights, fears that the sacrifices in the war had been in vain and hatred for the perpetrators of the defeat seized him. Possessed by another vision, he made his final vocational choice: "There is no making pacts with Jews; there can only be the hard: either--or. I, for my part, decided to go into politics."(30)

The striking feature of the decision was its ecstatic, visionary quality. It is not surprising for a paroxysmal-paranoid to fall into trance states and like a medium become transfigured by unconscious forces. Even later, in the 1930's, after he had come to power, visiting diplomats would be astonished by Hitler's trances. It was particularly apparent in his oratory. As one recalls: "These 'fits' might last ten minutes or a half hour or even three quarters of an hour. He seemed exhausted; it was as though his batteries had run dry."(31) His oratory was like the Cain event.

An equally prominent aspect of the Pasewalk decision was the intense anti-Semitism. Until he joined the army, Hitler was not especially anti-Jewish. While in Vienna, he read racist pamphlets and engaged in excited political debates. That he was not a rabid anti-Semite previously only means that his vocational choice was still in the making.

The psychological significance is that the relative suddenness of the identity change presupposes a compulsive choice of an expedient ideology. Earlier he lacked any ego content by which to justify his inner needs. But to an unstable paroxysmal-paranoid anti-Semitism is an appropriate vehicle for a personal identity and emotional outlet. Consequently, as early as 1919, only a few months after his decision, he articulates an extremely radical anti-Judaism in a letter:

> Rational antisemitism ... must lead to a systematic and legal struggle against, and eradication of, what privileges the Jews enjoy over other foreigners living among us (Alien Laws). Its final objective ... must be the total removal of all Jews from our midst.(32)

In this statement the environmental ideology coheres with the traumatic upbringing and lethal heredity into a radically unfree fate pattern.

B. **Friendship Choice.** After the war, Hitler joined the fledgling German Workers' Party which he hoped would be a vehicle for his new political career. As soon as he entered this group, the members recognized his leadership and oratorical talent. Using the party as a platform, Hitler harangued the people about the love of the nation and the hatred of the Jews. Eventually, his hypnotic power attracted hundreds into the party.

We do not need to recite the well-known history of the Nazi ascent. What is necessary is to point out some of the dynamics within the Hitler circle. Since the party evolved as a Cain brotherhood, socializing the passions of the unemployed and the disenchanted, it could not be called intimate in a familial sense. The loss of the war was so traumatic that all classes, all kinds of people, were radicalized. The anxiety aroused by the war facilitated the expression of various kinds of personal disorders.

The people who worked closely with Hitler have been described as psychopathic, socially maladjusted, or politically naive. Ernst Röhm was a well-respected soldier, a sexual pervert, and a veteran of front-line combat. Hermann Göring had been a famous pilot and exhibitionist; he would become a drug addict. Rudolf Hess was a shy, retiring idealist. Julius Streicher was an anti-Semite, a sadist, and one who publically carried a whip, as did Hitler. Joseph Göbbels saw in Hitler a messianic firebrand and eventually became his propaganda chief.

These and others came to Hitler out of fascination. Perhaps they could not articulate why they joined the party. Their choices were made compulsively and ecstatically, thus suggesting bonds that would lead to destructive fates rather than creative destinies. Consistent with the unfree quality of the decisions, Hitler kept his inner circle in fragments. Personally aloof from all, he confided fully to no one. Instead he cultivated a world of hatred, intrigue, and mistrust.

Albert Speer has recalled that the most frequently heard term in the Third Reich was "loyalty."(33) Surely this was not a description of faithful trust in a great leader. It was an introjection of a father figure in order to mask internal discontent, both sexual and emotional, an insecurity that could burst outward at any time in violent homocidal fury against their brothers. For the Hitler circle was an apocalyptic brotherhood whose first love was death and destruction.

C. **Marriage Choice.** One of the clearest insights into the dynamics of Hitler's cruelty may be found in his relationships with women. Many women were attracted to him, often hysterically. For much of his life he avoided marriage and particularly desired not to have children. But in the few hours before his death, he revealed a rare moment of tenderness and agreed to marry his mistress Eva Braun. He "decided to take that girl for my wife who after many years of sincere friendship freely entered the beleaguered city to share her fate with mine."(34)

Behind this belated marriage lies a history of tragic affairs with other women. His first teen-age love was a girl named Stephanie who lived in his home town of Linz. She became the unknown object of his love only from a distance. Even though Adolf never made actual contact with her, he maintained his passionate and imaginative crush on her.

In 1925, after becoming a public figure, he fell in love with Mitzi Reiter. She was 16, he 36. The age discrepancy resembled his parents'. Hitler compared Mitzi's eyes to his mother's and, one day, daringly asked her for a kiss. She refused but later recanted. Whereupon he became aroused and said: "I want to crush you."(35)

A few months later Hitler met his niece Geli Raubal and totally fell for her. Out of jealousy Mitzi attempted suicide. Yet Hitler remained attached to Geli and invited her to live with him in Munich. She agreed, but she found life with her famous uncle constricting and abnormal. Once she confessed to a friend that her uncle was a monster. She said: "You would never believe the things he makes me do."(36)

The "unbelievable things" were apparently coprophiliac perversions. In the original psychiatric report to the United States Army, Walter Langer has explained the significance of these perversions: "It is an extreme form of masochism in which the individual derives sexual gratification from the act of having a woman urinate or defecate on him."(37) Not only did Hitler command Geli to perform these perversions, but Eva Braun and probably his other mistresses as well.

While Hitler was living with Geli, he met Eva Braun who was originally an assistant in Hoffmann's photography studio in Munich. The press meanwhile hinted of incest in Hitler's family. In 1931, Hitler suddenly confronted a serious personal crisis. One day Geli was found lying dead on the floor, a 6.34 caliber pistol at her side. Geli's suicide triggered a profound melancholy and humiliation in Hitler, the same depression he felt on the death of his mother. He reacted to this crisis with a new burst of activity and inflative paranoia, telling a Munich crowd in the 1932 elections that God was on his side.

It is surely ironic that the master of the Third Reich could only relate to women incestuously and perversely, precisely in the hour of his meteoric rise to power. At the same time, Hitler was reveling in sexual anecdotes about the nature of politics. He once said to Ernst Hanfstaengl that politics is "like a harlot; if you love her unsuccessfully she bites your head off."(38) Similarly, in defiant rage, he frequently would boast about his enemies that heads could roll.

D. **Illness.** When Adolf Hitler finally became the Chancellor of Germany on January 30, 1933, he stood at the climax of an unprecedented political career. To commemorate his stunning rise to power the SS and SA troopers conducted a sparkling torch light parade, marching in awesome cadence amid dazzling search lights penetrating the dark sky. Standing alone above the hysterical crowds was the Führer, possessed by elemental forces, and perhaps envisaging with blazing eyes the apocalyptic fires soon to ignite the cities of the earth.

Hitler regarded his triumph as a matter of destiny. While such a claim is common among eminent historical figures, we now have in Szondian psychiatry a precise theory of destiny. One of the clearest ways to understand a man's destiny is to examine his illnesses and compare them to his major decisions. The possibilities of a destiny largely grow out of the inherited, learned, and traumatic pathological factors.

Adolf Hitler was generally free of serious organic disease. But he did suffer a class of ailments which some would call broadly psychosomatic. As an adolescent he had respiratory troubles and later, in his adult years, he incurred intestinal problems, hysterical blindness, and hypochondria. He interpreted his trembling and heavy perspiration as a cancer, a belief that was a part of his hypochondria.

These disturbances are traceable to unconscious emotional conflicts and are clinically related to the paroxysmal drive. They function as secondary defenses against the cumulative Cain affects whose energy boiled throughout Hitler's life. Although these

60

problems may exhibit a neurosis, they do not entail an advanced mental illness in the sense of a psychosis. Hitler was able to operate in social and historical reality.

However, at a much deeper level we can uncover serious personality disturbances of a different sort. Clearly Hitler was the bearer of a complicated psychopathology which would be classified clinically as a borderline condition between neurosis and psychosis. His psychopathology was instrumental to his career, because it reflected similar conflicts in those who were attracted to him. More precisely, the psychopathology can be interpreted as a function of splitting or disintegration of the basic personality drives.

Following the theory of disintegration developed by Szondi, we can briefly summarize what seem to be the major patterns in Hitler:(39)

1. **Contact Disintegration.** After the death of his mother he exhibits periodic depression followed by restless manic activity. These mood swings are activated by a personal crisis, such as a suicide attempt of a mistress. The depression is a symptom of clinging to the lost mother. The mania is an attempt to break all bonds and defend oneself against the depression. The character traits of contact disintegration are activism, a deep sense of inferiority, and dependent behavior--all of which Hitler shows at one time or another. In the causality of the depression the influence of the early childhood frustration is greater than that of heredity.

2. **Sexual Disintegration.** Evidence for this lies in his coprophilia and sado-masochism. The actual splitting means that, on the one hand, he shows an inability to be tender to anyone--until the time of his marriage. On the other hand, his aggressive need comes out, both in his savage political policies and in his masochistic self-punishment through the coprophilia. The disintegration manifests a rough, uncouth character and an obsessive defense in the form of fascination for incest and pornography. The origin of the sexual disintegration is mainly the crippling, overindulgent, and anxious childhood treatment by the mother as well as beatings by the father.

3. Paroxysmal Disintegration. Hitler is also an example of pure evil. He combines the Cain emotions with an exhibitionism. But a pure Abel is lacking. For he fails to experience guilt and a need for restitution. The closest he comes to the Abel side is a vulnerability to anxiety and to the previously mentioned psychosomatic disturbances. Paroxysmal disintegration also grows out of environmental influences like parental beatings and family deaths. The critical years for paroxysmal discharges are three to four and six to eight.

4. Mental Disintegration. This kind of splitting is rare, because it is usually found in advanced psychotics. As a pre-psychotic, Hitler does reveal a paranoia and a life-long self-destructive pattern. With the former he relies upon projection as a permanent way of coping with crises. Constantly, he blames others for his mistakes, fails to achieve self-insight, and needs to live with enemies. The latter is an unconscious use of the ego mechanism of negation. In everything Hitler attempts, whether in school, art, personal relationships, and eventually politics, he fails. This suggests a life-long need for self-destruction.(40)

All of these forms of disintegration indicate respective dangers in Hitler's personality. Since they add up to a self-destructive pattern without restitution, we can see these altogether as a psychological portrait of the demonic. Similarly, they who were attracted to Hitler, who saw in him their deliverer from the same conflicts, were destined to perish with him. So we conclude this chapter by illustrating how a paroxysmal-paranoid completes his destiny.

E. Mode of Death. In April, 1945, the twi-light of the Third Reich was at hand. The Nazi forces had been unable to halt the advances of the allied armies. The Russians and the Americans were driving toward Berlin, where Hitler remained hidden in an underground bunker.

The sound of Soviet shelling became so loud that Hitler was not able to sleep. At noon on April 22, having been aroused by the furious fire power, he listened to a discouraging report on German losses and allied advances. Suddenly, he stopped listening and screamed.

That's the end! Under such circumstances, I can't direct anything anymore! The war is lost! But you are mistaken gentlemen, if you think I will leave Berlin! I'd rather put a bullet through my head.(41)

The either-or quality of his outburst is the kind of interpretation we expect of a disintegrating personality. But the suicide threat was hardly the first one in his life. The first threat appeared in his adolescence, when he feared his imaginary lover Stephanie was ignoring him. He threatened not only to jump into the Danube River but also to take her with him in a love-death covenant. What is significant is that he chose a body of water as the means. For this method is most frequently chosen by paroxysmal types.(42)

The second threat came during the 1923 Beer Hall Putsch in Munich, at a moment of confusion when failure appeared imminent. Another threat followed in 1932 after the Nazi Party lost more than two million votes in the national elections. In the following month, factions broke out in the party and Gregor Strasser accused Hitler of being Satanic. Still another threat came on November 23, 1939, when Hitler shocked his generals by ordering a full scale war on the Eastern and Western fronts. The generals were reluctant to accept Hitler's order, because Germany was industrially unprepared for extended combat.

In each of these instances the suicide threat is posed in a crisis of victory or defeat. Faced with others' resistance or afflicted with his own depression, Hitler releases an outburst of Cain passions against himself. Amid the crisis Hitler shows a moment of inhibition or indecisiveness before the discharge of manic aggressiveness and suicidal rage.

The final suicide threat in 1945 was no different than the predecessors. This is not difficult to understand, in as much as suicide often shows a history of threats or attempts, particularly when the person is acting out of a fate pattern. But Hitler's moment of death has remained controversial. The traditional view held that he shot himself with a pistol on April 30, 1945.

However, the conclusions of the Soviet autopsy on Hitler's corpse, discovered after an abortive cremation attempt, indicate that cyanide poisoning was the actual cause.(43) The Soviet physicians found a bullet lodged in Hitler's left temple; yet it had drawn no blood. He was therefore poisoned first and shot second. Since his left arm was weak, he probably could not have held up a pistol to the side of his head.

While historians debate who shot the Führer, whether Eva Braun or his valet Heinz Linge, what is clinically significant is the mode of death. For poison and pistols often go together as suicide means. They are most frequently chosen by paranoid persons.(44) So whether he died by poison or by a bullet is not psychologically crucial. In either case he died as he had lived since his childhood.

The literary evidence for Hitler's paranoia is found in his "Political Testament," which he dictated at the end of his life. He declares in a series of erroneous projections that neither he nor "anyone else in Germany wanted war in 1939. It was wanted and provoked solely by international statesmen either of Jewish origin or working for Jewish interests."(45) He concludes his statement with a request to his successors "to resist mercilessly the poisoner of all nations, international Jewry."(46)

So in the early morning hours of April 30, 1945, Adolf Hitler completed his fateful life. From the beginning until the end, Hitler's destiny unfolded in a consistent pattern of unfree choices and personal disintegration. Inherent in his fate was a life-long push toward self-destruction, a climax also shared in apocalyptic horror by all those who saw in his hypnotic oratory the deliverance from their suffering.

Footnotes

1. Cf. Richard Rubinstein, The Cunning of History (New York: Harper, 1975), pp. 22-28.

2. Stanley Milgram, Obedience to Authority (New York: Harper, 1974), pp. 133, 145-146.

3. Hannah Arendt, Eichmann in Jerusalem (New York: Viking, 1964), p. 135.

4. John Steiner, Power Politics and Social Change in National Socialist Germany (The Hague: Mouton, 1976), p. 155.

5.   Heinz Höhne, The Order of the Death's Head, trans. by R. Barry (New York: Coward-McCann, 1970), pp. 9-12.

6.   Paul Tillich, "Das Dämonische," Gesammelte Werke, Band VI (Stuttgart: Evangelisches Verlagswerk, 1963), pp. 41-42.

7.   L. Szondi, personal correspondance, August 23, 1979.

8.   John Toland, Adolf Hitler (New York: Ballantine, 1976), p. 337.

9.   Adolf Hitler, Mein Kampf, trans. by R. Manheim (Boston: Houghton Mifflin, 1943), p. 5.

10.   Robert Waite, The Psychopathic God (New York: Basic Books, 1977), p. 171.

11.   Emanuel Lugert quoted in Franz Jetzinger, Hitler's Youth, trans. by L. Wilson (Westport: Greenwood, 1976), p. 44.

12.   Ibid.

13.   Quoted in Toland, op. cit., p. 8.

14.   Rudolph Binion, "Hitler's Concept of Lebensraum," History of Childhood Quarterly, I:2 (Fall, 1973), pp. 187-188, 192-193.

15.   Waite, op. cit., p. 164.

16.   Hitler, op. cit., pp. 42-44.

17.   Phyllis Greenacre, "Perversions," The Psychoanalytic Study of the Child, XXIII (New York: International Universities Press, 1968), p. 56.

18.   Szondi, Die Triebentmischten, p. 132.

19.   Quoted in G. M. Gilbert, The Psychology of Dictatorship (New York: Ronald, 1950), p. 18.

20.   L. Szondi, Freiheit und Zwang im Schicksal des Einzelnen (Bern: Hans Huber, 1968), p. 92.

21. Jacques Brosse, Hitler avant Hitler (Paris: Fayard, 1972), p. 106.

22. Jetzinger, op. cit., p. 68.

23. August Kubizeck, The Young Hitler I Knew, trans. by E. Anderson (Westport: Greenwood, 1976), pp. 114, 134.

24. Ibid., pp. 17-18.

25. L. Szondi, Schicksalsanalyse, Dritte Auflage (Basel: Schwabe, 1965), pp. 149-150.

26. Kubizeck, op. cit., p. 100.

27. Ibid., p. 153.

28. Werner Maser, Hitler's Letters and Notes, trans. by A. Pomerans (New York: Harper, 1974), p. 90.

29. Hitler, op. cit., p. 204.

30. Ibid., p. 206.

31. Andre Francois-Poncet, The Fateful Years, trans. by J. Leclerq (New York: Harcourt Brace, 1949), p. 291.

32. Maser, op. cit., p. 215.

33. Albert Speer, Spandau, trans. by R. and C. Winston (New York: Macmillan, 1976), p. 192.

34. Maser, op. cit., p. 205.

35. Toland, op. cit., p. 289.

36. Ernst Hanfstaengl, Unheard Witness (Philadelphia: Lippincott, 1957), p. 170.

37. Walter Langer, The Mind of Adolf Hitler (New York: Basic Books, 1972), p. 134.

38. Hanfstaengl, op. cit., p. 147.

39. Szondi, Die Triebentmischten, pp. 142-143.

40.   James   McRandle,   The   Track   of   the   Wolf
(Evanston: Northwestern, 1965), p. 155.

41.   Lev Bezymenski, The Death of Adolf Hitler
(New York: Harcourt, Brace & World, 1968), p. 12.

42.   Szondi, Freiheit und Zwang im Schicksal des
Einzelnen, p. 27.

43.   Bezymenski, op. cit., p. 49.

44.   Szondi, Freiheit und Zwang im Schicksal des
Einzelnen, p. 27.

45.   Maser, op. cit., pp. 346, 349.

46.   Ibid., p. 365.

Chapter Five: THE FAILURE OF ATONEMENT

I.   Violation of the Human Order

The suicide of Adolf Hitler was not so much the end of an era as a beginning.   More than eleven million had reportedly perished in the Nazi concentration camps.   Though many of Hitler's victims were Jewish, we should not forget that Christians were also enemies of the state.   The Nazi era created an ongoing theological crisis for Christianity, because Hitler claimed to be a messiah and his party an eschatological cult.(1)   He wanted to exterminate the entire Hebrew-Christian tradition and replace it with his own world view.

The Nazi program perpetrated a radical violation of the universal human order, that is, the law of participation which the doctrine of Creation upholds. The biblical vision of the world created by God stood in the way of a crude materialistic metaphysics which lay at the heart of Hitler's plan of genocide.   For in his scheme history is an unlimited life-death struggle for limited space against those who espouse a universalism or trans-spatial identity.(2)

The Nazi space is further defined by the Nordic race, the bearers of an ideal physiognomy.   People whose biological characteristics deviate from the Nordic ideal are to be eradicated.   Behind this foreign policy lies Hitler's assumption that the natural evolution of a group proceeds in its own gene pool without mixture or cross-breeding.   The political struggle for space requires a purification of the breeding ground.

We now know that Hitler's understanding of biology was wrong.   The mixture of the races strengthens the universal gene pool.   This is affirmed theologically by the fact that the Christian covenant with God includes all mankind.   Hitler's genocide was an assault upon the doctrine of Creation, because he failed to make restitution for his crimes.   Yet following the logic of Creation, atonement must be made.

The ethical problem of Hitler's aggression is quite clear.   Whenever in the act of evil atonement is not made, then the aggression is non-paroxysmal.(3) It is not difficult to identify the non-paroxysmal modes of aggression which Hitler has bequeathed to us. Their respective psychological correlates are found in Hitler's personality. They are each indicated by a disintegration of the basic drives in his destiny. As Hitler grew older, sadism, paranoia, and depression became more dominant; they occupied the interpersonal foreground of his personality. Meanwhile the Cain passions, so prominent in his childhood, became more hidden, functioning as background energies for his overt actions.

A. **Sadism.** One of the most obvious forms of non-paroxysmal aggression, in Hitler and his associates, is sadism. Though it may co-act with the Cain event, it is primarily a sexual or lustful need to control persons through cruelty. Hitler's sadism increased toward the end of his life the more he masochistically and perversely submitted to his mistresses.

B. **Frustration-Aggression.** Another form derives from a disintegrating contact drive. We become frustrated when we are dependent upon another person but do not feel genuine acceptance. To get acceptance we lash out at the person. Such frustration obtains from childhood insecurity and depressive loss.

Hitler was frequently depressed, and he often reacted to it with increased military action. This illustrates the fact that frustration-aggression leads to terrorism. The danger of terrorism is that it is not easily socialized; it is simply racial or class rataliation.

The 1938 Enabling Act is an example of the non-sublimated quality of terrorism. This decree abolished all rights and privileges of Jews in Nazi Germany. It replaced constitutional law with ideology, certain directives that resulted in the concentration camps. The denial of constitutional law is the consequence of terrorism in the form of state power.

C. **Necrophilia.** In his own study of Hitler, Erich Fromm has proposed the concept of necrophilia to account for a special kind of destruction. He defines this as a passion to destroy all life and an attraction to a dull, lifeless, mechanized routine.(4) Necrophilia is present in the love of technology, bureaucratic efficiency, and in manipulative marketing practices. This condition may have a genetic predis-

position of the schizoform type and in its pure
clinical form exhibits autism.

In Fromm's use necrophilia is actually a mental
disintegration. One turns away from the rich world of
persons and acts out of an abstract, unfeeling, cal-
culating manner. One example of a necrophiliac would
be Adolf Eichmann. During his 1961 trial, the Israeli
psychiatrist I. S. Kulcsar gave the Szondi Test to
Eichmann. The results, along with the subsequent
consultation with Szondi, set forth a clear profile of
a criminal psychopath.

Eichmann's interpersonal life included sado-
masochistic perversions, enormous homocidal intent,
bisexual feelings, projections of blame, and an
autistic power ego in the sense of Fromm's necrophilia.(5) Underlying these patterns is a reservoir
of raw Cain emotions, masked by an obsessive clinging
to the bureaucratic structure. When Hannah Arendt saw
Eichmann as a banal figure, she overlooked the
surcharged paroxysmality lying in the background. But
her controversial observation at least illustrates how
dangerous bureaucracies can be; they help to camou-
flage, at the expense of legal restraints, the
administrators of sadism, terrorism, and rational
destruction.

II. Chronic, Senseless Pain

Though he bore the Cain emotions, Eichmann
executed primarily a non-paroxysmal aggression in his
dictatorial rule. The horror of his place in history
is that he too inflicted evil without restitution.
Research on the Holocaust is now in progress, and the
results, published by survivors and scholars, may
never be conclusive. But some reference to the
ethical predicament, however risky and tentative,
should be included in a theological study of good and
evil.

We can draw an analogy with unatoned evil by
recalling some aspects of the experience of pain. In
current theory, it is no longer possible to think of
pain as a simple reaction to a noxious stimulus. Pain
involves a complex interaction of sensory impact,
cognitive interpretation, personal and cultural
motivation. The threshold of pain tolerance varies
with cultural and religious backgrounds.(6)

As long as we can believe in a moral universe, we can tolerate serious pain. One example is a deeply religious person who dies serenely after a long bout with cancer. Another would be Oriental mystics who flog themselves into heights of ecstasy. Still another is a football player who plays a rough game with a broken leg. All of these persons have an integrated sense of meaning which nullifies the pain.

But a problem arises when the pain lasts for a long time, and the moral framework collapses. Chronic pain is less manageable, less clear in its signals. The world of chronic pain has been compared to that of a nightmare. According to one clinician, both have three characteristics:

1. The individual undergoes a reign of terrible things. 2. One is trapped by these forces and loses control. 3. The sense of time, of an orderly succession of past, present, and future breaks down.(7) Instead of a coherent process, experience becomes a chaos of discrete, disordered moments.

The breakdown of time by chronic pain helps to erode the moral framework and increase the mental suffering. As the universe disintegrates, the pain itself becomes a world view. We can only scream in abject anguish. The cry threatens our dignity and sometimes forces us to regress back to childhood, when we first looked upon the world as a place of terror.

These clinical insights seem to be analogous to what survivors have felt in the beginning of their confinement. A survivor of Auschwitz recalls:

> A desolating grief is now born in me, like certain barely remembered pains of one's early infancy. It is pain in its pure state, not tempered by a sense of reality and by the intrusion of extraneous circum-stances, a pain like that which makes children cry ....(8)

The cry erects a barrier against any rational-istic theodicy. Appeals to an orderly universe, a process metaphysics, or a theology of hope cannot penetrate to a primal affliction as unatoned, chronic pain. Concentration camps are a monument to cruelty which has no purpose and no immediate redemption. In this vein, Elie Cohen explains, on his arrival in a camp, that he went into a depersonalization when he saw a guard beating a man for no reason.(9)

Cohen goes on to note that in long-term imprisonment, after the initial shock, ordinary psychosomatic symptoms disappear. Asthma, ulcers, eczema, high blood pressure, and diabetes pass away in this boundary line condition.(10) They normally appear in civilization as symptoms of unresolved emotional and moral conflicts. But in trans-moral confinement these defenses are replaced by chronic infection, malnutrition, diarrhea, and exhaustion.

The passing of the paroxysmal symptoms is also connected with the decline of suicide. One simply lacks the energy to kill oneself. In some respects, suicide can be considered as a kind of "restitution," a way of working out ethical conflicts. But suicide has no promise, because it lacks a real atonement.

Behind the unregenerate nightmare of the camps stands a glaring political fact. Adolf Eichmann formulated a policy of deliberate cruelty, an alternation of sadism and sympathy.(11) The intent of his policy was to create confusion and undermine all personal defenses. He was so proud of his work that, at the end of the war, he exclaimed: "I can joyously jump into my grave, knowing my mission has been fulfilled."(12)

III. Pervasive Psychic Numbing

The Nazi period stands out primarily as a prototype of Cain event, sadism, terrorism, and necrophilia. But in the same year that Hitler died, on the other side of the world, a radical assault took place, one that also undercut the act-fate structure of atonement. We conclude this chapter by referring to the atomic bombing of Hiroshima. While this has no association with the Nazi policy, it nevertheless represents a mode of rational destruction which has some similarities with necrophilia.

Hiroshima is an obstacle to any theory of destiny, because it was the site of a total and unexpected strike. Christian missionaries had been working in the city, and the people thought their presence was a benevolent sign. But with that fateful hour on August 6, 1945, a life-long survivor process was set in motion. The nature of this process has been reconstructed by Robert Lifton.

A. **Total Immersion in Death.** According to Lifton, the shock of the bomb made a permanent death imprint.(13) Afflicted by this ad hoc introjection, the survivor would become the carrier of a basic anxiety, losing all sense of invulnerability. Common to this trauma was the belief that the entire world had perished in a monstrous experiment. Whereas the city had once been lively and productive, now it lay barren and silent beneath the blue-green flashes of fire that danced against the dark sky.

To cope with the shock, the people underwent a psychic numbing. This is a chronic closure of the organism that blocks out threatening stimuli. The closure includes a loss of feeling, impairment of thinking, and a withdrawal of contact with the social world. The state conforms to what is usually known as a war neurosis. For the Hiroshima survivor, a shrinking away from experience was the only way to handle the overwhelming death threat.

B. **Invisible Contamination.** Since toxic radiation was a serious effect of the bomb, there also arose a widespread belief that the bombing poisoned all of nature.(14) This fear was confirmed by actual poisoning and disfigurement and by imaginary radiation. Lifton even found that long after 1945, the survivors continued to blame the bomb for any illness, even though a causal connection could not be made.

C. **A-Bomb Disease.** Along with imagined radiation, survivors did contract a high rate of cancer.(15) This also raises the possibility of genetic mutations which may be transmitted in families for several generations. This, combined with the global concern for nuclear testing and accidents, has caused us to realize that the lethal effects of technological destruction cannot be confined to an immediate historical period. Lethal effects are virtually unlimited.

D. **Identification with the Dead.** Out of the ashes of the city, the survivors came forth as a group, bound in a mystic solidarity and tainted with shame. They have become a new minority, suffering the fears and biases of larger populations.

74

Their solidarity is based upon a total identification with the dead.(16) The identification seems to be a desperate clinging to a broken set of bonds, which is a disintegration of the contact drive resulting in chronic depression. The need for acceptance is transferred to the dead in an introjected shame. Consequently, the survivor feels profound guilt. One wonders why they died not he or she. Why am I alive? Am I not alive at their expense? This survivor guilt is so deep that the survivor feels that he or she has no right to exist. Instead they behold the dead as sacred and pure.

The Hiroshima survivors suffered a serious crisis after the war. When President Harry Truman was asked if he had any regrets for ordering the bombing, he said no.(17) Learning of this admission, the Japanese felt great hatred for the American government. To many Americans the Cain reaction may not have been entirely clear.

The reason is that in Japan it is proper to express feelings of regret over a death.(18) It does not matter whether one were uninvolved with it. The regret demonstrates that we have suffered an inexorable event, a fate beyond our control. Without the initiation of regret there is no emotional basis on which restitution can be made. So the process of rage and shame, hatred and guilt persists.

The danger of technological destruction is that the administrators are faced with a probable psychic numbing of their own. The enormity of technology severs human feelings from the operations. While Harry Truman cannot be compared to Adolf Hitler, nevertheless the tragedy of each demonstates what happens when technology is a means of foreign policy. The aggression is likely to become non-paroxysmal and therefore obstruct the cyclical process of atonement.

Footnotes

1. John Steiner, **Power Politics and Social Change in National Socialist Germany**, pp. 110-113.

2. Eberhard Jäckel, **Hitler's Weltanschauung**, trans. by H. Arnold (Middletown: Wesleyan University, 1972), p. 94.

3. Szondi, Die Triebentmischten, p. 163.

4.   Erich Fromm, The Anatomy of Human Destructiveness (New York: Holt, Rinehart, and Winston, 1973), p. 332.

5.   I. S. Kulcsar, et. al., "Adolf Eichmann and the Third Reich," Crime, Law, and Corrections, ed. by R. Slovenko (Springfield: Charles C. Thomas, 1966), p. 45.

6.   Ronald Melzack, The Puzzle of Pain (New York: Basic Books, 1973), p. 25.

7.   Lawrence LeShan, "The World of the Patient in Severe Pain of Long Duration," Stress and Survival, ed. by C. Garfield (St. Louis: C. V. Mosby, 1979), p. 274.

8.   Primo Levi, Survival in Auschwitz, trans. by S. Woolf (New York: Collier, 1973), p. 54.

9.   Elie Cohen, Human Behavior in the Concentration Camps, trans. by M. Braaksma (New York: Universal Library, 1953), p. 116.

10.   Ibid., pp. 64-65.

11.   Nora Levin, The Holocaust (New York: Schocken, 1973), pp. 119-120.

12.   Quoted in Kulcsar, op. cit., p. 18.

13.   Robert Lifton, Death in Life (New York: Random House, 1967), p. 21.

14.   Ibid., p. 57.

15.   Ibid., p. 103.

16.   Ibid., p. 201.

17.   Ibid., p. 334.

18.   Takeo Doi, The Anatomy of Dependence, trans. by J. Bester (Tokyo: Kodansha, 1973), p. 122.

Chapter Six: LOSS AND POWER

I. Survival and Bereavement

Survival--writes Elias Canetti--is an experience
of power.(1) The passage through brutality and terror
is so momentous that it makes us utterly unique. As a
power, the survivor's uniqueness is stronger than
grief. For it turns into a confidence of invulnerability, often becoming a craving for more and more
power.

Canetti's linking of survival and power is
provocative, since the victims of terror are commonly
seen in their powerlessness. But if, on the other
hand, the perpetrators of radical evil have been
unable to make amends for their crimes, may not this
failure signify a powerlessness in the rulers of the
world? Certainly, the connection of power and
survival is fitting, because the same theme appears in
the literature. Primo Levi explains the power of
survival as a refusal to be reduced to the level of
beasts.(2)

But there are two uncertainties about Canetti's
insight. What is the exact nature of the power which
survival exhibits? And is the experience of survival
separable from grief? The difficulty with the second
problem is that several autobiographies of survivors
refer explicitly to grief. Alexander Donat, for
example, tells how the people in the concentration
camps discussed things without emotion during the day
but grieved at night: "alone in the dark, we wept,
and in the morning arose with tears still undried,
fragments of our nightmares still clinging to us."(3)

Robert Lifton also demonstrates that victimization "can be associated with prolonged grief and
mourning.... The early symptoms he experiences have
been described as characteristic for 'acute
grief'...."(4) Grief may be defined as the subjective
reaction to the loss of a relationship in which one
has experienced dependency. Classical psychoanalysis
has also shown that the pre- and post-trauma states
may involve ambivalence.

The grief reaction includes not only recurrent
feelings of bodily distress but also shock, numbness,
possibly panic and anger, and usually disbelief. The
bereaved may suffer guilt and hatred, become preoc-

cupied with a mental image of the deceased, and identify with the normal and abnormal behavior of the one who has died. As time goes by, the bereaved may experience periodic separation anxiety, often taking the form of dreams and visions. While yearning for the deceased may not be consoling, the bereaved may even suffer occasional delusions, hallucinations, and depersonalization.(5)

There is no uniform pattern of bereavement. We grieve in our own ways. Whatever the nature of the loss, the bereaved must cope with it. Certainly, the natural temptation is to avoid the loss, withdraw from life, and deny the death. But this can only lead to despair and personal disorganization. So-called abnormal grief is a sign that the bereaved has avoided coping with the loss and has remained fixed on a particular stage in the grieving process. For example, we may cling to shock, hatred, or depression.

The task of coping is called grief work. It is commonly experienced in three broad phases:

1.   The physical reality of the death is accepted. This is particularly important in cases of sudden death. For until we see the corpse, we may not actually believe death has happened.

2.   The bereaved expresses the Cain emotions. Discharging these affects, while weeping, is a way of allowing ourselves to adjust gradually to the loss. Weeping especially lowers the level of consciousness, so that we can let the knowledge of the loss sink in. The repeated crying and talking about the death, in all the details, help us to disengage from the deceased. We must gradually divest ourselves of emotional attachments and come to appreciate the deceased objectively.

3.   Eventually, we must also achieve a balanced outlook on the person who has died, including both the positive and negative qualities. This will enable us to resume living and to re-establish new relationships, even though we remember that no one can replace the deceased. While the symptoms of grieving should pass away, the memory of the person should not.

The essence of grief work, therefore, is recollection. The process has been confirmed clinically and is also known to the religious traditions. In the Hebrew tradition recollection is

> zakhar, to remember, call to mind, commem-
> orate. When the soul remembers something,
> it does not mean that it has an objective
> memory image of some thing or event, but
> that this image is called forth in the soul
> and assists in determining its direction,
> its action.(6)

The recollection is of a transcendent or past reality.

In classical Greek thought recollection (anamnesis) is distinguished from memory (mneme). Plato defines in the Philebus recollection as the power of the mind to recover a truth that has been forgotten.(7) Memory is the consciously preserved relation with the truth. Through the memory the mind has the power to grasp the truth of being rather than the past. It is not a simple retention of a past event.

The Greek term for recollection is still used in therapy. It can also refer to the dynamics of grief work. Calling to mind, over and over again, the details of the death contributes to an acceptance of the loss and a renewal. The recollection varies in the length and symptoms according to the nature of the loss and the strength of the bereaved. But whatever form it takes, it remains basic to the destiny of the survivor.

II. Grief Work Amid Atrocity

In their memoirs, some survivors have testified to the grief in their experiences, thus contradicting Canetti's remark. But we should ask, as Canetti does not, about the grief work. It would seem that the continuing publication of autobiographies is an important part of a broad collective grief work conducted by the survivors. The telling and retelling of the horrors of Auschwitz and Hiroshima would seem to be a form of recollection.

But the psychiatric model of grief work is admittedly individualistic and may not be fully applicable to cultural movements. In order to test the applicability, I would like to draw a few brief parallels between the grief work model and the survival experience.

A. **Acceptance of the Death.** Even under ordinary conditions it is difficult to accept the fact that someone has died. But in the war whole populations and countless families perished. The sheer number of the dead virtually prevents a concrete acceptance of the fact of death. What has been called the "body count" functions as a dehumanizing cliche, when attempting to quantify the dead.

B. **Detachment from the Dead.** In ordinary experience one or two years may be required to complete the grief work. Yet after its completion, a survivor may undergo periodic anniversary reactions. But when one's entire family perished in Nazi ovens, the emerging survivor guilt tends to prevent such a detachment. The identification, which Lifton found in Hiroshima, further erodes the possibility of an emotional reinvestment in new relationships. Consequently, a clinging to the dead may be a permanent feature of grieving during atrocities.

C. **Renewal of Relationships.** What is astonishing about the post-war period is that the survivors have, after all, survived. Because of this miracle, the twentieth century survivors have spoken of power. Chaim Kaplan has poignantly expressed the paradox: "We live broken and shattered lives; lives of shame and dishonor; lives of suffering and grief. But the power of adaptability within us is miraculous."(8)

Kaplan's insight touches down to the negative paroxysmal-hysteroid factor, the tendency to hide one's face in the moment of awesome danger. But this inclination is inherently moral, and the feelings of shame, guilt, and grief co-act with the Abel tendency in a plea for restitution. So while the on-going discussions of the Holocaust command us to remember, the grievous shame of the survivor actually affirms a new and profound moral power.

III. Three Kinds of Power

What is the power that rises from the depths of shame? Is it not the power that comes from the fundamental law of participation? Since all persons are endowed with this basic relational function, then the power to participate is given in biological descent, in the genes. Though threatened with crises, our struggle to survive re-activates the law of participation even at the crude biological level.

But this power to be is expressed through several drives. It can be manifest in our aggression, our contact-bonding, our imagination, as well as our passions of rage and shame, anger and guilt. Even in the radical states of depersonalization and acute abnormal grief, the fundamental drives are present in the background of each person. As long as they are in the background, they can rotate into the interpersonal foreground.

Because human tendencies are complex, it is necessary to consider that the experience of power is not a simple matter. Power too is complex.

A. **Virtual Power.** In our struggle with crises it is known that we often engage in projection. But projection is not inherently bad. There are times when the transfer of unconscious content onto another plane of reality enhances a relationship. One example is love, wherein a lover projects feelings of tenderness upon his beloved. Such a projection is participatory.

The value of projective-participation is not entirely practical. It is—to borrow an idea from Susanne Langer—virtual.(9) The transfer of feeling creates a domain of meaning and value that transcends everyday life. The projected sphere is more symbolic than physical. But the virtual realm, when penetrated, can release a formidable power. Often virtual power is discharged in meditation, music, dance, or writing, particularly in times of solitude.

A compelling example of virtual power and survival has come out of the Soviet prison system. During the 1930's, Eugenia Ginzburg was arrested by the Soviet state and sentenced to ten years of solitary confinement. For the first few years, she was able to visit a library and read the works of the great Russian poets. Within two years, she felt that the confinement had deepened her sensitivity.

> I reflected once again on the power which literature exerts on us in that state of spiritual composure which prison life

induces, and which makes us strive, devoutly
and humbly, to drink in an author's words to
the full.(10)

At the end of her term, she was re-sentenced to
an additional eight years in a labor camp. Seeing how
degrading the camp was, she realized how ennobling her
prison solitude had been. For the last years of her
ordeal she remembered the dignity achieved in her
previous solitude. This was the only way she endured
the terror of the Soviet system.

B. **Unilateral Power.** Another way of surviving
is to become aggressive, particularly against an
opposing force. This entails unilateral power, which
may be defined as "the ability to produce intended or
desired effects in our relationship to nature or to
other people."(11) The unilaterally acting self
pursues specific goals often in a manipulative manner.
Since the goals are usually quantitative and measured
in terms of success, this force is a power of having
rather than being. The voluntary aspect of the ego
combines with the aggression of the sexual drive in
the struggle to survive.

To illustrate this kind of power, we may recall
that during the war as many as two million Jews
escaped destruction by the Hitler regime. They chose
the means of armed and unarmed resistance.(12)
Aggressive action was particularly effective at the
edge of the Nazi empire. At a Benedictine Convent,
near the Vilna Ghetto of Poland, a Mother Superior
organized her sisters into an underground movement.
She had been disturbed by the Nazi terror and wanted
to make contact with the people in the ghetto.

During the winter of 1941, the Mother Superior
decided to assist the newly established Jewish
Fighters' Organization. She "roamed the countryside
in search of knives, daggers, bayonets, pistols, guns,
grenades. The hands accustomed to the touch of rosary
beads became expert with explosives."(13) Not only
did she exhibit unilateral power but she also became a
source of spiritual renewal.

Although she worked selflessly, tirelessly,
she felt not enough was being done. "I wish
to come to the ghetto," she said ... "to
fight by your side, to die, if necessary.
Your fight is a holy one. You are a noble
people ... you are closer to God than I."(14)

C. Relational Power. While the virtual has been active in solitude, and the unilateral in the liberation struggle, a third form has emerged in the degradation of the concentration camps. All the primary sources agree that survival is a communal act. No one has survived alone. Only they who help one another, not necessarily out of tenderness or compassion, can make it in the boundary-line conditions. This conforms to what has been called relational power: "The ability both to produce and to undergo an effect.... The capacity both to influence others and be influenced by others."(15)

This form of power exhibits the elasticity of the contact drive, the capacity to bind and separate, give and take. The irony of relational power is that the more we endure the impact of evil affects the more we increase in moral stature. In this dramatic give and take the relational self seeks neither success nor bigness. The aim is to forge an internal relation with the other and to maintain it amid great adversity.

In advanced cases of survival, relational power may be more adaptive than the other two. Lena Donat has made this point. "I did not see; I did not hear; I did not want to see or hear or know. I wanted to live ... I had already developed a heart of stone and nerves of steel ...."(16) Following this admission of an aggressive unilateral power, she continues: "all that only served to facilitate my survival, not to guarantee it; actually I survived Auschwitz because some merciful hand protected me."(17)

So out of the horror of Hitler's Reich a profound horizon has emerged. The exercise of relational power, in the struggle to survive, has revealed a transcendent perspective. The frail, emaciated bodies of survivors, stepping out of the ashes of fallen worlds, bear witness to a new form of restitution. They have met the radical assaults of evil in the most sinister forms. Their achievement leads us to open up the question of an appropriate theological response.

Footnotes

1. Elias Canetti, Crowds and Power, trans. by C. Stewart (New York: Viking, 1962), p. 227.

2. Levi, Survival in Auschwitz, p. 36.

3. Alexander Donat, The Holocaust Kingdom (New York: Holt, Rinehart, and Winston, 1963), p. 261.

4. Lifton, op. cit., p. 483. For survivors' statements about grief see Cohen, op. cit., p. 159; Levi, op. cit., p. 54; Abraham Katsch, ed., The Warsaw Diary of Chaim A. Kaplan (New York: Collier, 1973), p. 74; Miklos Nyiszli, Auschwitz, trans. by T. Kremer and R. Seaver (Greenwich: Fawcett, 1960), p. 160; Irving Rosenbaum, The Holocaust and Halakhah (New York: KTAV, 1976), pp. 68-75.

5. Avery Weisman, "Coping with Untimely Death," Psychiatry, 36 (Nov., 1973), p. 371.

6. Johs. Pedersen, Israel: Its Life and Culture, I (London: Geoffrey Cumberlege, 1926), p. 106.

7. Plato, Philebus, 34.

8. Katsch, op. cit., p. 86.

9. Susanne Langer, Feeling and Form (New York: Charles Scribner's Sons, 1953), pp. 40-50.

10. Eugenia Ginzburg, Journey into the Whirlwind, trans. by P. Stevenson and M. Hayward (New York: Harcourt Brace Jovanovich, 1967), p. 228.

11. Bernard Loomer, "Two Kinds of Power," Criterion, 15:1 (Winter, 1976), p. 14.

12. Philip Friedman, Their Brothers' Keepers (New York: Schocken, 1978), p. 13.

13. Ibid., p. 26.

14. Ibid., p. 27.

15. Loomer, op. cit., p. 20.

16. Quoted in Donat, op. cit., p. 304.

17. Ibid., p. 365.

Chapter Seven: THE STRUGGLE FOR ATONEMENT

I. Meditation and Virtual Power

The awesome spectacles of evil in the twentieth century have seriously threatened the Hebrew-Christian tradition. When Christianity enters into a crisis, it becomes necessary to rethink the fundamental themes of the faith. Such a task falls to theology. A systematic articulation of the Christian faith is stimulated by contemporary experience and conducted within the context of Scripture and tradition.

Not surprisingly, many theologies have appeared in the twentieth century. But only those which are deeply grounded in experience, along with the Bible and tradition, should be taken seriously. One of the theses of this book is that the Cain complex is an appropriate tool in the analysis of experience. It combines biblical and scientific insight in a penetrating grasp of evil. Even where evil shows a non-paroxysmal form, as in radical destruction, the Cain complex still offers a valid set of criteria.

The struggle against evil has involved a sequence of radical loss and astonishing power. Our analysis shows that three kinds of power are present in survival. These are rooted in the basic drives and are connected to the quest for value and restitution. For the forms of survival power are deeply moral. Survivors themselves appeal to the world community in order to prevent further Holocausts. This appeal presupposes the needs for value and restitution.

It therefore seems appropriate to classify current theologies in terms of their attention to the moral aspects of survival power. This is to suggest that theology, in its ethical and experiential bases, be measured by the atonement of the Cain event and its equivalents. This further implies that the respective theologies, in order to grasp experience, should come to terms with the forms of power.

An appeal to virtual power has been helpful to intellectuals or artists threatened with the crises of survival. Choosing virtual power can unfold in a contemplative destiny. We can find theological versions of virtual power in the religious experiences of contemporary Japan. The Hiroshima bombing has forced Christians there to rethink the meaning of their faith. Much of the Christian-Buddhist dialogue is devoted to this task.

Among Christian theologians, the pilgrimmage of Hugo Enomiya-Lassalle has been inspirational. This German-born Jesuit was one of the missionaries in Hiroshima during the war. As early as 1942, he was a student of Zen Buddhism. In that year he conducted a personal retreat at a monastery. Since then, he has continued to meditate in the Zen style, while still remaining a priest and a Christian. He survived the atomic bombing and has become theologically influential.

Enomiya-Lassalle has written extensively on meditation. In one book he explains that many Christians, both lay and clerical, have had some difficulty in praying. Having suffered the terrors of war, they have not been able to integrate a theistic vision of God with radical evil.(1) I believe he is referring to those trained to pray in a classical manner, as expounded, for example, by St. Ignatius Loyola in his Spiritual Exercises. In this method we are to imprint images of suffering on our mind's eye, be deeply moved by them, and act with contrition.

But if a survivor is afflicted with psychic numbing, it may be difficult to pray that way. Robert Lifton has shown that the survivor's greatest problem is in finding the right images to piece the world back together again. Numbing blocks our ability to symbolize the world of experience. This may be the reason why Enomiya-Lassalle prefers the "image-less" technique of Zen. In this mode one prays by sitting, breathing in a slow, controlled rhythm, and emptying the mind of all words and pictures.

This Christian Zen master defends this method as ethical. The contemplative is governed by this command: You do not sit for yourself.(2) We sit for others in order to purge our Cain emotions. The extinction of rage, hatred, and envy is a prominent theme in Buddhism as well. Once we dissolve our Cain emotions through meditation, we may then act out of love, justice, and harmony, which are the Abel emotions.

False meditation, in contrast, does not escape ego-centricity. True meditation resolves the Cain predicament and achieves a participation with God.

But the experience is non-conceptual, non-imaginal; it is simply felt. As in the classical mystical theology, the contemplative loves but does not conceive of God.

The destiny of Enomiya-Lassalle is a courageous testimony to a new form of theology. He witnesses to a restitution by means of virtual power. But the question we must raise is whether meditation provides a comprehensive answer to the problem of evil. The reason is that meditation is for the healthy and not the sick. Meditation is not psychotherapy. But Lifton's research in Hiroshima has shown that the survivor's grief may become a serious illness that is immune to meditation.

In fact, a completion of grief work may depend upon how we interpret the cause of evil. If we believe the crisis comes from God, then we may accept it as a judgment. Our belief in a moral universe is maintained. But if we see that the evil comes from human callousness or sheer exploitation, then our grief may turn into chronic despair.(3) Sensing no reason for the destruction, we may slide into a hopelessness and suffer a catatonic condition. This can be preserved for several generations in the family and local culture.

Such chronic grief would indicate a mental disintegration in the clinical form of an advanced inhibition. A disintegrating ego is prone to despair and self-destruction and loses the capacity to meditate. Tragically, the only recourse to a resolution may be a pseudo-restitution like suicide or drug abuse.

II. Liberation and Unilateral Power

When the twentieth century is viewed from the standpoint of power, a strange irony appears in the post-war period. The two world wars were mainly the products of modern nation-states jockeying unilaterally for power in the guise of territorial expansion. The wars were thus crises of unilateral power. But in the aftermath of the second world war, the same unilateral power also became manifest in the smaller countries of Asia, Africa, and Latin America.

Much of post-war history has been a struggle against colonialism. Larger nations had entered smaller countries in search of wealth and labor, imposing foreign languages, customs, technologies, and educational methods on the people. All of these had to be assimilated at the expense of traditional forms of participation in the world.

An acute analysis of the colonial situation has been presented by the Algerian psychiatrist Frantz Fanon. He has exposed colonialism as a dichotomy of the settler and the native.

> The settler pits brute force against the weight of numbers. He is an exhibitionist. His preoccupation with security makes him remind the native out loud that he alone is master. The settler keeps alive in the native an anger which he deprives of an outlet ....(4)

The settler reinforces a closed chamber of anger by maintaining the traditional tribal divisions and appeasing the old chiefs.

The exhibitionism and the triggering of the Cain emotions expose colonialism as a scene of paroxysmal disintegration, a pure evil. Since the settlers close off emotional outlets, the natives can only turn their Cain passions inward in fratricidal terror. Fratricide has been a prominent activity in twentieth century African politics. This turns attention away from the fact that the colonial assault upon the people is a Cain initiative.

The closed colonial system reinforces the traditional tribal mythologies. With mythic forms the people can transfer their fear and anger away from themselves. The projective-participation in the tribal mythology creates a symbolic domain of magic and intrigue. Whereas in industrial society a projective-participation might lead toward an autism, in the African tribal environment it is a source of identity.

But at the same time, the projection could not still the deep-seated emotional conflicts brought on by the colonial system. Fanon observed the natives' children becoming homocidal, suffering noise phobias, enuresis, insomnia, and sadistic desires.(5) Adults were vulnerable to ulcers, nephritic colitis, menstruation problems, insomnia, premature whitening of the hair, paroxysmal tachycardia, and muscular stiffness.(6) These disturbances are derived from the constant fear of death.

The colonial regime also used torture to get the natives to talk. One technique is to cross the pain threshold as quickly as possible with beatings, high pressure enemas, cigarette burns, anal insertions of bottles, and forced standing in awkward positions. These tortures result in the indifference to moral appeals and the non-rational suffering of an injustice. The same consequences can be found in the Nazi concentration camps.

Fanon's description clarifies the sources of the revolutionary impulse. The people unleash their Cain passions, aggression, and will to live onto the invaders. In view of the police torture it is likely that the revolutionary aggression may be sadistic. For sadism can be triggered by trauma. The mixture of the sexual aggression and the Cain passions unifies the people into a profound apocalyptic ecstasy.

The Algerian experience represents a shift from virtual to unilateral power. Formerly lethal passions were discharged through dance, mystic possession, and fratricide; now they inform direct action against the oppressor. The revolutionary assault becomes a mystic retaliation. Should the uprising become homocidal, then--so the reasoning goes--the colonial masters are getting what they deserve. For the natives argue that it is the settlers who first brought violence and death into the land.

Since the 1960's, the revolutionary motif has assumed a theological form. In response to the colonial predicament and to the previous Nazi oppression, liberation theology has set out to articulate the experience in Christian symbols. Oppression corresponds to evil, liberation to salvation. Alienation is seen as the condition of sinful existence. The hope of the oppressed is that the love of God be present with them in the struggle for freedom. Their liberation will atone for evil.

The great merit of liberation theology is its integration of the Christian faith with concrete experience and its confrontation with the Cain event. Though the forms of this theology vary culturally, they maintain the vision of atonement in their

struggle against evil. Liberation theology is the
heir of the resistance movements in the Nazi period.
But in the post-war era the object of the struggle is
economic inequality, as in Latin American thought, or
racism, as in Black theology.(7)

Nevertheless, liberation theology is vulnerable
to criticism, when appreciated in terms of the Cain
complex. Since freedom is measured by the resolution
of the Cain complex, we should ask whether liberation
theology can genuinely accomplish that task. One
prominent characteristic of such theology is the
readiness to bear arms and, thus, to reject nonviolence.(8) The appeal to violence is justified on
the grounds that the revolution requires whatever
means are necessary.

Such a tactic implies that the freedom struggle
is defined in terms of class retaliation. Violent
means are to repay violent grievances. But by making
means and ends identical, revolutionary theorists are
bound to an order of necessity. For the use of arms
tends to be repeated with a crude sameness that
threatens to erode the conscience and vitality of the
bearer.(9) The exchange of blood and fire power goes
on without cessation.

Liberation theology is also troubling psychologically. It often involves a public display of rage
and resentment. An exhibition of the Cain emotions in
theological books threatens a disintegration of the
paroxysmal drive. The result is that we observe a
two-fold exhibitionism: a large number of publica-
tions claiming liberation along with the expression of
outrage--but meanwhile little genuine freedom follows.

This kind of splitting leads us to wonder whether
the current liberation movements have brought about
any ethical advancement since the death of Hitler. Or
do we remain caught in the dilemma of the Cain
predicament?

III. Nonviolence and Relational Power

While in the 1930's the world anxiously watched
the rise of the Nazi Party, another revolutionary
movement was arising in India. Mohatma Gandhi was
developing a technique known as **Satyagraha** or "truth
force." This was a means of nonviolent resistance in
order for rural people to organize themselves in

opposition to urban industrialists. Having set out to defend the simple manufacturing processes of the villagers, Gandhi triggered a movement that led to the independence of India from the British Empire.

The image of a skinny but saintly figure, clad only in a simple loin cloth, leading unarmed marchers into the blows of police, broke new ethical ground in the twentieth century. The movement of public marches, boycotts, submission to hostile resistance, and even going to prison manifests a rich set of ethical values. It is partly a form of exhibitionism, but mainly it represents a pure Abel model: releasing the emotions of goodness, justice, and love while suffering the shame and fear of being beaten.

The theological version of nonviolence was represented by Martin Luther King Jr. He adopted Gandhi's technique and led the American Civil Rights movement in the 1950's and 1960's. King went beyond Gandhi by grounding the technique in Christian theology:(10)

A. **Active Resistance.** Though the technique employs unarmed demonstrators, it wields considerable aggression in the community against evil. Participants are bound together in a brotherhood and are capable of great relational power.

B. **Reconciliation.** The ideal is to reconcile the oppressed and the oppressors, seeking to subdue the perpetrators of evil without killing them. This represents a unified sexual drive.

C. **Defeat of Evil.** Since the aim is to conquer evil, people are not treated as enemies. This concept maintains a unified paroxysmal drive, because the technique clearly envisions restitution.

D. **Acceptance of Suffering.** The crucial test is to suffer without retaliating. Members of the Civil Rights movement were trained to fall on the ground, roll up like porcupines, and receive the assailants' blows. The weapons often consisted of rifle butts, baseball bats, and cattle prods. The marchers assumed that their oppressors would become nauseated by their cruelty. Being repelled, they were to recoil from their aggression, achieve moral insight, and repent of their evil. The repentance could come at any time, now or in the future.

E. **Avoidance of Spiritual Violence.** In contrast to liberation theology, King recommends the rejection of hatred. "In the struggle for human dignity the oppressed ... must not succumb to the temptation of becoming bitter or indulging in hate campaigns."(11) In place of the Cain affect, King appeals to the New Testament theme of agape love. He defines love as an active will to affirm the other's good and to restore community. "To the degree that I harm my brother, no matter what he is doing to me, to that extent I am harming myself."(12)

F. **Ultimate Love.** Nonviolence theology makes love ultimate. For King the cosmos is personal and interrelated. So justice is inherent in the nature of things. This means that the struggle against evil is in touch with reality. By appealing to an ultimate justice, King achieves a projective-participatory relationship with God. This establishes a transcendent framework in which the contact, sexual, and paroxysmal drives are affirmed without serious disintegration.

Thus, King seems to go the furthest, as a theologian, toward the restitution of the Cain predicament. His movement lacks the breaking apart of the drives which liberation theology may promote. But there is one fateful flaw in King's logic. His trust in the self-generating atonement of the racist assailant assumes a normal personality. If, however, the racist aggression generates a lust for destruction, a sadism, then his assault is not paroxysmal. A sadistic racism does not move toward insight or restitution.

We must therefore acknowledge that the bearer of a nonviolent theology may die by assassination. The murders of Gandhi and King are consistent with the destinies of those who march against evil in the world.

Footnotes

1. Hugo Enomiya-Lassalle, Zen unter Christen (Graz: Styria, 1973), pp. 13, 23.

2. Ibid., p. 33.

3. Robert Lifton and Eric Olson, "The Human Meaning of Total Disaster," **Psychiatry**, 39:1 (Feb., 1976), pp. 13-19.

4. Frantz Fanon, The Wretched of the Earth (New York: Grove, 1965), p. 43.

5. Ibid., p. 226.

6. Ibid., p. 237.

7. Gustavo Gutierrez, "Two Theological Perspectives," The Emergent Gospel, ed. by S. Torres and V. Fabella (Maryknoll: Orbis, 1978), p. 240; James Cone, Black Theology and Black Power (New York: Seabury, 1969), p. 32.

8. Colin Morris, Unyoung, Uncolored, Unpoor (Nashville: Abingdon, 1969), p. 94.

9. Jacques Ellul, Violence, trans. by C. Kings (New York: Seabury, 1969), p. 91.

10. Martin Luther King, Jr., Stride Toward Freedom (New York: Ballantine, 1958), pp. 81-86.

11. Ibid., p. 83.

12. Ibid., p. 85.

Chapter Eight: VICTIMIZATION AND REVELATION

I. Jesus' Paroxysmal Ministry

Judging theology in terms of the Cain complex is a risk that requires an ultimate validation. By what authority may the Cain-Moses polarity be used theologically? Such a proposal should come out of a source wherein the atonement of the Cain event occurs on an ultimate level. This means that if the Cain complex would enter into theology, it must become an instrument in the understanding of divine revelation.

For Christian theology the principle of authority is found in the New Testament. This document witnesses to a revelation of God which is the norm for our life and faith. Appealing to the New Testament does not invalidate the authoritative self-disclosures of God in the Hebrew Scriptures. Neither can be separated from the other. The Covenant initiated with Jesus not only renews that made with Moses but offers a unique contribution.

Since the original atonement of the Cain event has been correlated with the Mosaic Law, the restitution consists of a divine initiative. God intervenes in bestowing a sign on Cain and in making the revelation through Moses on Mt. Sinai. The Mosaic structure of atonement is therefore as valid for Christianity as it is for Judaism. But where Christianity differs is in the crucifixion. While Jesus resembles Moses in some respects, he does not actually kill a man. Jesus is murdered instead.

Although Jesus did not murder, he did shed some Cain emotions. The Gospel writers, particularly the Synoptics, portray Jesus as a paroxysmal personality. The historical background of Jesus' Cain qualities was Jewish apocalypticism. As a prophet he intended to confront Israel with the expected end of the world. Jesus criticized the people and yet identified with them. He was a Jew speaking to other Jews in the same way that members of a family love, admonish, and even quarrel with one another.

The apocalyptic context is particularly vivid in Mark. He wrote the earliest Gospel to narrate the rule of God, the defeat of the hostile demonic powers, and to outline the shape of the community for the world situation.(1) Mark portrays Jesus as one who

95

proclaimed the coming of the Kingdom of God, healed the sick, and cast out demons. Mark was sensitive to the fact that the Hellenistic aristocracy of Jerusalem exercised an oppressive influence among the poor. The dominance of the wealthy classes was a kind of demonic pressure.

In his own struggle against the demonic forces, Jesus became possessed by coarse Cain emotions. Mark chapter one makes this clear in Jesus' healing of the leper.

> And he sternly charged (embrimesamenos) him, and sent him away at once, and said to him, "See that you say nothing to any one; but go, show yourself to the priest, and offer for your cleansing what Moses commanded ...." (Mk. 1:43-44a)

The phrase "sternly charged" is a weak translation for the Greek term, which conveys great anger in the sense of a snorting, bucking horse. Jesus' Cain emotions are released like a surgeon's scalpel, cutting out the demonic affliction and restoring wholeness to the person.

Mark chapter three goes on to explain how Jesus saves a man with a withered hand. He heals on the Sabbath and is accused of violating its sacredness. In reply he claims that healing carries on the intent of the Sabbath.

> And he looked around at them with anger (orges), grieved at their hardness of heart, and said to the man, "Stretch out your hand." He stretched it out, and his hand was restored. (Mk. 3:5)

The Greek term for anger conveys enormous wrath.

The irony of Mark 3:5 is that Jesus grieves as he rages. In fact, his wrath is mixed with weeping throughout his ministry. This tells us that Jesus is psychologically balanced. Within his paroxysmal nature the epileptoid and hysteroid, Cain and Abel, emotions are integrated. Whenever his Cain intensity stands out, his Abel tenderness lies in the background. Because Jesus combines Cain and Abel feelings, he is capable of great ecstasy. "And when his friends heard it, they went out to seize him, for they said, 'He is beside (**ekseste**) himself.'" (Mk. 3:21)

While Mark illumines the Cain aspects of Jesus' healing, Matthew reveals them in his teaching. Matthew draws a general, though not exact, comparison between Jesus and Moses. Both are called teachers. Jesus' contribution to the Mosaic legacy occurs primarily in the Sermon on the Mount.

> You have heard that it was said to the men of old, "You shall not kill; and whoever kills shall be liable to judgment." But I say to you that every one who is angry with his brother shall be liable to judgment .... (Matt. 5:21-22a)

In this passage Jesus identifies the Cain event but emphasizes that the motive in itself is lethal. Just to feel anger, envy, vengeance, hatred is to commit a sin. The same applies to adultery, divorce, swearing falsely, and retaliation, which are equivalents of the Cain event. While the Ten Commandments prescribe atonement for these acts, Jesus renews the judgment and emphasizes mainly the Cain motive.

However, a shift of emphasis takes place at the end of the fifth chapter. Jesus says of the Law:

> You have heard that it was said, "You shall love your neighbor and hate your enemy." But I say to you, Love your enemies and pray for those who persecute you .... (Matt. 5:43-44)

This summation does not actually appear in the Hebrew Scriptures, but it does in the sect of Qumran. A current scholarly judgment is that this phrase represents Matthew's criticism of sectarian Judaism.(2) The profound psychological truth in Jesus' utterance is that hating the enemy prevents a resolution of the Cain complex.

But yet the subtle irony of these passages is that Jesus judges exactly what he experiences. Does this not invalidate his prophetic destiny? Surely not; for in order to heal the people afflicted by the Cain emotions, he must be able to experience them in himself. Otherwise his relationship with the demons would lack power; his ministry to the people would be insensitive.

At the same time, Jesus is acutely aware that his ministry is provocative:

> Do you think that I have come to give peace on earth? No, I tell you, but rather division; for henceforth in one house there will be five divided, three against two and two against three; they will be divided, father against son and son against father, mother against daughter and daughter against her mother .... (Lk. 12:51-53a)

Jesus does not preach what ought to happen as a result of his ministry. He indicates the practical fact that paroxysmal forces will probably be conjured up in families. This insight presupposes the act-fate structure of human experience.

The fateful consequences triggered by Jesus' ministry may lead some scholars to emphasize his tragic destiny. Did not the Greeks regard tragedy as a rehearsal of the deeds of great men who ventured beyond the limits of ordinary experience? They clearly understood that the heroes provoked resentment and envy in the common people, causing them to rebound and destroy the great men. Knowing that the arrogance of the heroes was the precipitating factor of their downfall, the Greeks used this motif in the theatre to remind the audience of their own mortality and nobility.(3)

But Greek tragedy was concerned with the Oedipal problem, with the murder of the patriarch and the desire for the mother, the seeds of this conflict ripening in the course of several generations leading eventually to the destruction of the heroic descendants. For the Greeks, tragedy occurs within the family.

In contrast, the Gospel goes in a different direction, toward the Cain predicament. This can be seen when Jesus was told: "'Your mother and your brothers are standing outside, desiring to see you.' But he said to them, 'My mother and my brothers are those who hear the Word of God and do it.'" (Lk. 8:20-21) Jesus broadens the family into an apocalyptic brotherhood and sisterhood. This conforms to the psychological fact that the resolution of the Cain complex takes place in a social group outside the family. Coming to terms with the brother originates a brotherhood.

The Gospels also ascribe healing functions to Jesus' brotherhood. The disciples are sent out on the road, without money or supplies, as "sheep in the midst of wolves," encouraged to be "wise as serpents and innocent as doves." (Matt. 10:16) If faced with persecution, they are not to fight but to flee. Jesus clearly defines the role of his brothers non-heroically.(4) His appeals to danger and vigilance refer to the paroxysmal startle function. For this reason it is a mistake to interpret Jesus' ministry as an example of human sexuality.(5) Jesus certainly expresses love and compassion toward the brothers and sisters of his community. But these are Abel emotions set in the context of intrigue, murder, and terror.

Thus, Jesus' apocalyptic actions are thoroughly paroxysmal. His rage and grief are moral emotions. They are what we ought to feel when we see evil and injustice. The task of the apocalyptic prophet is to mediate the struggle against evil and witness to God's transcendent defeat of the demonic forces.

With the rise of liberation theology in recent years, students of the Bible have been concerned with the means of the apocalyptic conquest. Did Jesus sanction violence in the struggle? Was his brotherhood a revolutionary vanguard planning to overthrow the Temple system? Was he associated with the Zealot terrorists?

That Jesus was openly hostile to the Jerusalem establishment is well-known. Matthew chapter 23 extols Jesus' stinging Cain attack on institutionalism and entrenched aristocratic power. But whether Jesus advocated violence and the overthrow of the established political and priestly structures are matters of dispute. A conventional argument for Jesus' alleged appeal to violence would be based upon his cleansing of the Temple, after arriving in Jerusalem. He

> entered the temple of God and drove out all who sold and bought in the temple, and he overturned the tables of the money-changers and the seats of those who sold pigeons. He

said to them, "It is written, 'My house shall be called a house of prayer'; but you make it a den of robbers." (Matt. 21: 12-13)

To understand this passage theologians could benefit by a simple lesson in biology. Cleansing the Temple is hardly an act of violence, because no one is killed. Instead it is a display of aggression. Biologists define aggression as the use of force to defend a territory against an opponent. This is a constructive force that seeks to subdue but not destroy the other. The purpose of aggression is to protect a bond within the species. By analogy, Jesus exercises aggression to restore the divine-human Covenant as staked out in the territory of the Temple. His cleansing is simply a benign mixture of paroxysmality and aggression.

But while Jesus is in the city, he does expound the apocalyptic vision of the end of the world. He envisages that the end will bring about great conflict, persecution, and suffering. With colorful imagery he describes the Messiah dispatching his warrior-angels to the ends of the earth. Yet he keeps his vision open-ended, not tying it down to a specific date. "But of that day or that hour no one knows, not even the angels in heaven, nor the Son, but only the Father. Take heed, watch ...." (Mk. 13:32-33a) Once again he urges vigilance.

We can imagine these messages sending shock waves throughout the alleys and market places of Jerusalem. Probably the Zealot terrorists, disguising themselves and their knives in the crowds, took Jesus' oratory as a signal to start the apocalyptic holy war.(6) The long awaited warrior-Messiah had at last arrived--they reasoned--and now was the time to strike. The Zealots wanted to overthrow the Temple cult and priesthood with a new religious structure. Their program meant that the Mosaic Law, and the belief in the coming Kingdom of God, would be defended by murder.

But the signals received by the Zealots, the Jewish priesthood, and even the Romans remained confusing. They had heard Jesus proclaim the coming Kingdom; but they had never heard him urge killing anyone. Jesus had denounced the Cain passions of greed, hatred, deceit, and injustice. Amid these diverse perceptions of Jesus, perhaps the Romans felt threatened and the Zealots excited. But the terrorists could not have been sure how they were to assemble, with Jesus presumably leading them, to begin the holy war. Jesus did not act. He did not arrange to meet the Zealots.

Probably Judas, who was a Zealot, decided to arrange for Jesus' arrest by a Roman cohort in order to force him into action. But something went wrong. Jesus did not resist the seizure. And when a disciple raised his sword like a Zealot ready to attack, Jesus forbade him. His rejection of the sword caused severe disappointment in Judas and the other Zealots. The remainder of the disciples became quite confused and even fled in panic.

Not all of the details of Jesus' abduction are clear. We may assume that the disciples did indeed run away, and that later Peter did deny his association with Jesus. The flight and the denial are simply natural defenses against the trauma of Jesus' arrest. Apparently, Jesus was taken to the residence of Caiaphas, the high priest. There he and the other members of the Jewish Court conducted an informal, emergency hearing, perhaps with the knowledge and consent of the Romans. Modern scholarship has effectively demonstrated that this session was not a formal or legal trial.(7) The priests wanted to learn something about Jesus' mission. They were agitated and upset.

Caiaphas begins by asking, "Are you the Christ, the Son of the Blessed?" And Jesus said, "I am; and you will see the Son of man sitting at the right hand of Power, and coming with the clouds of heaven." (Mk. 14:61b-62) The confession appears on the surface to be an acceptance of the Messianic title. But the "I am" has been disclosed, in terms of the Aramaic original, to be more like the following kind of answer: "You say that I am; and not I."(8) It is thus an evasive statement. Jesus therefore avoids a confrontation with the high priest.

Jesus' answer is quite revealing in a legal sense. If he had assented to being a Messianic figure, he could not have been convicted on Jewish grounds. For Hebrew law did not define Messianic claims as criminal. However, Caiaphas was surely aware of the fact that such a confession would be incriminating in Roman law. The Romans did convict felons engaging in violent or non-violent resistance against the state. Could it not be that the Jewish priests were trying to intercede on Jesus' behalf, either to understand his intentions or to change them?

What they found was an unco-operative Jesus. His conduct was not criminal by Jewish standards, nor could his reply be called a confession in Roman terms. The ambiguity of the situation mounted, so that Caiaphas exploded. "And the high priest tore his mantle, and said, 'Why do we still need witnesses? You have heard his blasphemy. What is your decision?' And they all condemned him as deserving death." (Mk. 14:63-64) Possessed by anger, they began to beat and spit on him.

This climax requires a close scrutiny. For the high priest alone to tear his clothing is unusual. In court procedure a conviction for a capital offense was signified by all members performing this act. Here only one does it. The action cannot be explained unless we look at Judaism as a whole. The only time in Jewish custom when one person rents his clothing is during the week known as shiva, when the family is grieving over a death, and the chief mourner tears his garments. Could not this mourning custom be applied to the Gospel scene?(9) If so, then we are able to comprehend the subtlety of the entire passage.

The priests' outburst against Jesus is an example of frustration-aggression. Having tried to help or understand Jesus, they were frustrated because they could not establish a relationship with him. Fearing perhaps that he would be tried and convicted by the Romans, they threw up their hands in angry resignation. The priests could only step back and let Jesus stand alone before the Roman state.

When they say he has uttered a blasphemy, this can only be taken as a non-technical cry of disgust. Blasphemy was technically defined as speaking the name of God outside the annual Day of Atonement ritual, an act reserved only for a priest. (Lev. 16) But references to blasphemy were made informally, and in this case Jesus was simply being sworn at in a crude way and not being charged with a legal offense.(10)

It is certainly possible for grief to turn into anger on certain occasions. When it happens, it shows an Abel-to-Cain turn about. Such an affect swing requires that the previous relationship between the two parties has been one of ambivalence. The break-down of an intensely ambivalent relation can easily trigger a Cain reaction. Jesus' ministry had evoked ambivalent reactions.

For Jesus defended the intent of the Mosaic Law with a vigor that exceeded Rabbinic standards, while simultaneously making savage criticisms against the religious and political institutions.(11) No wonder that the Jewish leaders had been aroused to such a love-hate intensity. When the Gospels say the latter set out to kill Jesus, they mean that the ambivalence had become virtually lethal by frustration.

For the people and the priests had projected their hopes of national renewal onto Jesus. But events were deteriorating and, suddenly, Jesus ends up in a Roman court, standing before the dreaded Pontius Pilate. This Roman prosecutor was reputed to be cruel and arrogant. At least once, between 26 and 32 A.D. when he ruled in Palestine, he was recalled to Rome and admonished for his domineering policies. As a legal officer, Pilate was responsible for prosecuting serious crimes. Were the accused a Roman citizen, he could transfer the trial to Rome. With a foreigner, he lacked the right of delegation. He had to try the case.

According to the **Lex Julia Majestatis**, the death penalty was decreed for insurrection against the state. This did not automatically entail crucifixion. The cross was reserved mainly for hard core criminals, robbers, and Roman citizens guilty of treason.(12) Robbers and criminals were usually lower-class types, and the crucifixion served as a deterrent. When the crucifixion was used, it was preceded by torture, usually flogging.

To understand the trial of Jesus, let us block out doctrinal considerations, for the moment, and think of the legal issues. Pilate was said to be brutal by historical testimony. But the Gospels see him as vacillating, reluctant to get involved. He even stands Jesus next to Barrabas, a hard core criminal and Zealot, and he asks the crowd to judge which one should be released, assuming this were customary during the Passover time. The crowd demands Barrabas to be let go, Jesus crucified. Modern scholarship has questioned whether the practice of letting out prisoners at Passover ever existed.(13)

But even if it were possible, consulting a crowd would contradict Roman trial procedures.

While Jesus may have been perceived by the Romans as a revolutionary, he was neither a hard core criminal, robber, nor traitor. So crucifying Jesus would have been out of proportion with his actual conduct. No political agency, no property, were seized by Jesus. He preached the coming Kingdom of God but did not actively facilitate its arrival. It would therefore seem that Jesus did not deserve to be crucified. He expected to die and to suffer, thereby departing from the Jewish understanding of the Messiah. But he probably did not expect to be crucified, because he could not have regarded his actions as criminal.

So the controversy comes down to a simple issue. Jesus was tried without due process and executed in an unjust manner. In only a few hours on a bleak day long ago, the brief career of Jesus came to an end in a disappointingly swift way.

II. The Crisis of the Crucifixion

Even though the cross was a political instrument, it satisfied deep-seated personal needs. Elevating a tortured, dying body on a cross, amid a crowd of excited bystanders, could not but deeply affect those who were witnesses. They were able to project their own feelings of vengeance, hatred, and rage onto the emaciated body.(14) By transferring their own Cain passions, the people were temporarily relieved of their fears of dying and suffering. Seeing someone else die in agony can be consoling to the insecure.

But the crowd vented more than Cain emotions. Since the crucifixion was preceded by torture, it was intended to induce a slow, agonizing death in the eyes of the people. The cross presented the humiliation and degradation of a helpless human being. We can only conclude that the public spectacle aroused fascination, lust, and sheer delight. It is similar to that feeling we get when we all gather on a street corner and excitedly watch a building burn to the ground and people jump from the windows to their deaths. Seeing pure destruction can bring out our latent sadism.

The crucifixion was therefore a mixture of Cain emotions and sadistic lust. As we have already seen, whenever the sadism dominates this blend, the Cain redemptive cycle is broken. The rage and hatred do not in themselves convert to insight or restitution. Governed by sexual lust, our Cain emotions can be quickly transported to a destructive rapture. When this ecstasy appears, so does the demonic.

While the Gospel writers describe the execution of Jesus as illegal, they are also making a profound political statement. Pilate's behavior is so contrived that his trial is outrageous. The entire scene should be read with tongue-in-cheek. For the Gospels are making a literary exaggeration in order to draw attention to the fact that Jesus' death was demonic, totalistic, and out of touch with moral and legal reality. The Gospels are assigning demonic properties to the state and making an unprecedented devaluation of established institutions. State power is exposed as ruthless and cunning.

My "Szondian" interpretation may illumine why the cross was so horrifying in antiquity. Jewish law, for example, forbade crucifixion, preferring stoning, hanging, or strangling as more humane means of a quick death. The cross was offensive to the Jews mainly because of its shamefulness and wretchedness. That it was equally traumatic to Jesus himself may be inferred from the fact that he died so quickly. His shock death presupposes that he did not expect to be crucified.

Jesus' crucifixion, like shock events in general, awakened in the Hebrew memory earlier traumas. It is the tendency of a crisis to disarm the defenses of the participants and cause them to recollect previous and more successful coping models. If we cannot handle a shock in the present, we go back to an earlier time and adopt a tactic that has already been helpful. The question posed by the cross, however, is what material does the shock re-enact?

We can get a clue to this problem by reading Galations chapter three. "Christ redeemed us from the curse of the law, having become a curse for us--for it is written, 'Cursed be every one who hangs on a tree.'" (Gal. 3:13) Although Paul wrote this passage several years after the crucifixion, the lapse of time does not matter. Once a trauma happens, in the experience of a people, it does not pass away from their memory. It may be forgotten temporarily and then re-surface in subsequent crises.

Paul's Galations passage recollects, in the Hebrew memory, the following verse:

> And if a man has committed a crime punishable by death and he is put to death, and you hang him on a tree, his body shall not remain all night upon the tree, but you shall bury him the same day, for a hanged man is accursed by God .... (Deut. 21:22-23a)

Paul is not quoting Deuteronomy exactly, because literary precision is not the issue. What matters is that the memory of one hanging on a tree now serves as a symbolic framework to work through the shock of Jesus' death. The Deuteronomy passage becomes fruitful in the grief work of the early Christian community.

The irony is that Paul refers to the cross as a curse. Surely this does not mean that Jesus is to blame for his own death in a strict act-fate manner. On the contrary, Jesus was not responsible for his own death; he was victimized. To call the cross a curse means that the projected Cain emotions and sadistic lust could not convert into a restitution. A natural atonement had not come about. So the crucifixion, by breaking the Cain cycle, opened up the need for a new kind of restitution. The death of Jesus set the stage for one more contribution to the legacies of Cain and Moses.

III. Restitution and Resurrection

We have known, since antiquity, that we are the most deeply moved by striking or grotesque images. Aristotle taught that the capacity to be moved was the meaning of **pathos** or passion.(15) The images of Greek tragedy have the power to evoke fear and pity, those of Greek comedy laughter and well-being. While the Gospels may at times make us laugh or weep, their central image does neither. The cross makes us shudder in devastating horror.

The crucifixion has lasted for centuries as a powerful image in the piety of the people. When considering this impact psychologically, there must be a reason for such endurance. The image of the cross has to penetrate unconscious needs and feelings in order to grasp the mind and heart. So the unconscious materials, which the Gospels presuppose, must be different than those reflected by comedy and tragedy. The Gospel is too serious for comedy and too ordinary for tragedy.

The latent pathos is the catastrophic fear of dismemberment, destruction, and mutilation. This fear is a negative blend of paroxysmal, sexual, and relational needs that we all have in our familial unconscious. The fear of dismemberment is a deep memory traceable to the pre-natal struggles of the fetus against danger.(16) The fear of being mutilated, of being chopped into pieces, goes deeper than that of mortal sickness or natural death. Because we preserve a primeval memory of dismemberment, we are susceptible to horror in the face of the cross.

It is precisely this latent stratum that informs our love of evil. One purpose of anxiety is to defend ourselves against this deep catastrophic feeling. This means that the redemption of evil requires a confrontation with the crucifixion image, or its equivalents, in order to discharge the energy of its horror and facilitate a cleansing ecstasy. But drawing the Cain-sadistic-brokenness blend from darkness into light cannot be accomplished by human insight or mental effort alone. It can only come from a transcendent divine initiative.

We can understand such an action by reading the Synoptic Resurrection narratives psychologically and reconstructing the grief work of the early Christians. Mark chapter fifteen shows the beginning of the process by recording Jesus' agony. "My God, my God, why hast thou forsaken me?" (Mk. 15:34b) According to Mark, Jesus recollects Psalm 22 as a way to comprehend his own alienation.(17) This suggests to us that the Hebrew Scriptures, particularly the Psalms, may have been helpful to the early Christians, as they had to contend with Jesus' abandonment and dismemberment.

But since the natural restitutive cycle has been broken, only God can draw the grief work to a conclusion. The completion of the grief work is implied in the declaration of the Resurrection. The significance of this announcement is not whether Jesus did or did not physically lift off from the grave. The debate over the physical details has occupied Christians ever since the second century. But what is important is the fact that Mark identifies certain emotions as equivalents of the Resurrection.

In chapter sixteen he describes three women coming to the tomb of Jesus, learning that he has risen, and then running away--"for trembling (tromos) and astonishment (ekstasis) had come upon them; and they said nothing to any one, for they were afraid (ephobounto)." (Mk. 16:8b) Having become speechless before an ineffable event, they were filled with fear, trembling, and ecstasy.

Were these not the same emotions felt by Adam and Eve in Eden, and Moses before the burning bush on Sinai? These feelings seem always to accompany those who become the bearers of a new transcendent relationship with God. The fear and trembling manifest the experience of religious value through the latent hysteroid side of human nature. The ecstasy indicates an expansion of the self to a genuine participation with God. With a restored transcendent relationship, the lethal and sadistic tendencies are overcome. The fear of mutilation is surpassed by a new communion. We are permitted to transfer our own Cain-sadistic tendencies toward the divine presence in the cross. This is the meaning of the second generation Pauline phrase: "Christ died for our sins." (I Cor. 15:3)

While Mark has illumined the psychological dimensions of the Resurrection, Luke has clarified the historical. That Jesus was executed in the city may have triggered the memory of Cain as the builder of the first city. Even the Zealots had hoped that the city would be the place where they would release their Cain passions in apocalyptic vengeance. But the forces of the city instead consumed Jesus.

In his Gospel Luke tells the story of two men walking on the road to Emmaus. They are joined by a stranger who in reality is Jesus. Not recognizing him, they nevertheless refer to his mission: "But we had hoped that he was the one to redeem Israel." (Lk. 24:21a) The three continue walking until they arrive at their destination. They sit down and break bread together. Precisely, at that moment the two recognize Jesus. But suddenly he leaves. He goes back to Jerusalem, where he greets his disciples. "And while they still disbelieved for joy, and wondered, he said to them, 'Have you anything here to eat?' They gave him a piece of broiled fish, and he took it and ate before them." (Lk. 24:41-43)

This simple story is highly symbolic, but it sets forth a new model of destiny based upon the Resurrection. The Greco-Roman world had perceived Jesus as a hero, a great man who, having died, left behind a memorable legacy and entered into the Pantheon of deities. But Luke contends in this story that Jesus was not a hero.(18) He had not gone away. Jesus had stayed in the world with his brothers and sisters, eating bread and broiled fish.

We can understand the Lucan vision of destiny by recalling how the Cain complex is resolved in society. They who overcome the Cain passions and achieve control of their destinies unite with one another in a new brotherhood. Eating bread and fish with the slain brother manifests a deeply felt concrete relationship. An oral introjection, which is more profound than mentally identifying with an idea, signifies the formation of a new character. Henceforth the people live and die in terms of the crucified one. They face catastrophic death with the trust that the law of participation is at work, keeping them in the divine presence.

Footnotes

1. Howard C. Kee, Community of the New Age (Philadelphia: Westminster, 1977), p. 70.

2. W. D. Davies, The Sermon on the Mount (Nashville: Abingdon, 1966), p. 83.

3. Charles Beye, Ancient Greek Literature and Society (Garden City: Doubleday, 1975), p. 338.

4. Stendahl, Paul Among Jews and Gentiles, pp. 49-50.

5. William Phipps, The Sexuality of Jesus (New York: Harper, 1973), pp. 10-14.

6. John Yoder, The Politics of Jesus (Grand Rapids: Eerdmans, 1972), p. 56.

7. Haim Cohn, "Reflections on the Trial and Death of Jesus," Jewish Law in Ancient and Modern Israel, ed. by H. Cohn (New York: KTAV, 1971), pp. 95-99.

8. John Knox, The Death of Christ (Nashville: Abingdon, 1958), p. 80.

9. Cohn, op. cit., p. 169.

10. D. E. Nineham, Saint Mark (Philadelphia: Westminster, 1977), p. 404.

11. Samuel Sandmel, Anti-Semitism in the New Testament? (Philadelphia: Fortress, 1978), p. 28.

12. Martin Hengel, Crucifixion, trans. by J. Bowden (Philadelphia: Fortress, 1977), pp. 34, 81, 83.

13. Paul Winter, On the Trial of Jesus, rev. and ed. by T. Burkill and G. Vermes (Berlin: Walter de Gruyter, 1974), p. 131.

14. Hengel, op. cit., p. 87.

15. Aristotle, Metaphysics 1022b and De Anima 432a.

16. Joseph Rheingold, The Mother, Anxiety, and Death (Boston: Little, Brown and Co., 1967), p. 80.

17. Hans-Ruedi Weber, The Cross, trans. by E. Jessett (Grand Rapids: Eerdmans, 1979), p. 36.

18. Norman Perrin, The Resurrection According to Matthew, Mark, and Luke (Philadelphia: Fortress, 1977), p. 66.

Chapter Nine: A TRANSCENDENT RECOLLECTION

I. The Need for an After-Life

Several centuries have passed since the end of the biblical period. Still the image of the crucifixion reverberates in the memory of our civilization. The age-old Christian task has been to proclaim and interpret God's restitution through the cross. In earlier times the announcement of the atonement, as embodied in the doctrine of the Resurrection, was confined to individual experience. Historically, the Resurrection has provided a pathway of the individual into a life after death.

In the twentieth century millions die at the whims of cruel and sinister tyrants. The age of radical evil has opened up a vision of virtually unlimited destruction. The century has indeed brought about a crisis for Christian theology, so much so that the quest for atonement must seek new forms.

Among contemporary thinkers one of the most comprehensive theories of restitution has come from John Hick. He has argued that the problem of evil can only be resolved by a belief in life after death. Evil must be revealed as rationally and morally integral to a future worth living.(1) Such a future goes beyond this present life span to include ages yet to come. Only this hope in a life after death enables most people in the world to conquer tragedy.

Hick contends that every person inherits at birth a tendency to grow toward perfection, toward a state of complete fulfillment. Our problem is that we lose the opportunity to become whole in the encounter with evil. So we need more than one lifetime to achieve perfection. What Hick envisages, therefore, is a pilgrimmage of the self through several life times, culminating in a final reunion with God.

The post-mortem journey of the soul

> occurs in a real spatio-temporal environment
> ... with its own laws ... real personal
> life--a world with its own concrete char-
> acter, its own history, its own absorbing
> and urgent concerns, its own crises ... and
> its own terminus ....(2)

He assumes that in ordinary experience we develop by struggling with the crises of an objective environment. By analogy, we should expect similar conditions after death.

Hick's position superficially resembles the traditional Asian doctrine of reincarnation. But he departs from that view when he affirms the doctrine of Creation. Instead of positing an endless cycle of pre-natal incarnations, he assigns an origin to the world. The advantage of positing a beginning is that it locates in nature the origin of good and evil. This permits us to determine where evil comes from, how we can combat it, and in what way we may recognize the good.

Hick argues that the Asian vision of unlimited births and rebirths simply postpones the problem of evil.(3) If I observe no origin to the world, and I claim that my evil was determined by actions committed before I was born, then I cannot come to terms with the causes. I cannot make restitution for something that has no determination within nature. For these reasons a doctrine of Creation grounds ethics in a theory of origins.

Even though Hick accepts Creation, he rejects the concept of the Fall. Mankind "did not fall disastrously from a better state into one of sin and guilt, with death as its punishment, but rather he is still in process of being created."(4) He sees death as merely one moment in the journey of the soul. Having been created in the image of God, we acquire a rational freedom and struggle with the ordeals of this world and the next until we enter into the mystery of God. The intermittent crises do not destroy the divine image; they develop it.

Hick's defense of freedom, his rejection of the Fall, and his claim for an origin of ethics accord with my thesis in chapter two. But in my view he does not precisely define the good, evil, and radical evil, nor the origin of good and evil. The value of the Cain complex is that it states exactly what good and evil are, and where in nature lies their origin. As we have said, radical evil is the non-paroxysmal aggression that goes beyond the Cain-Moses cycle of atonement.

In my reading of Hick's theory, evil is made instrumental to the full development of the soul. This is true in the sense that freedom is achieved in the conquest of the Cain complex. But when sadism, terrorism, and necrophilia break the restitution cycle, then no freedom obtains. The result is a pattern of self-destruction as illustrated in Hitler's tragic destiny. But Hick does not seem to consider this possibility.

Hick's argument about the perfectibility of finite freedom relies upon a process framework. He confidently claims that the tendency toward perfection is built into the biological organism.(5) The ideas of process and unlimited novelty appeal to many contemporary theologians. But whether a process vision of the self is fully compatible with scientific theory and the experience of evil is a matter of dispute. I disagree with John Hick on this point and suggest we pursue another path. For the cumulative experiences of scientists and survivors offer dissenting testimony.

The claim of perfection goes beyond what is admissible in modern biology. One of the clearest statements of how biology works may be found in the writings of Jacques Monod. He defends the established theory that life arises from chance. This concept paradoxically corresponds to the contingency of origins in the doctrine of Creation. Once forms are created they move in necessary patterns, unless interrupted by mutations. But the task of the species is to transmit the invariant characteristics of its forms.(6)

Nor can genetics be used to support an idea of human perfectibility. The entire drift of medical genetics is to uncover the hereditary roots of pathology. The practical consequence is that we are now pictured as the carriers of lethal genes, which may be transmitted for several generations. With the success of medical technology, particularly since the 1950's, more people are surviving birth and growing up to reproductive age. They are marrying one another and further transmitting lethal possibilities to their offspring.

Genetics moves not so much in a perfectionist way but toward a vision of tragic destiny. For even though we may inherit a wide range of possibilities, we scarcely choose them all. The tendencies listed in chapter one are a comprehensive number; but they rarely appear altogether in every person. The contribution of psychiatry is to confirm that normal existence is a matter of splitting. Many of us are lucky to live out the positive tendencies of the inherited drives. Many also fulfill the negative tendencies as well.

The fact of life is that free choice usually proceeds in a narrow manner. Only a few tendencies are chosen; meanwhile many remain in the background as unrealized potentialities. The common consequence of such limited choice behavior is that parents can be disappointed in their offspring. It is not only a destiny that separates us from animals; it is also our capacity to undergo tragedy.

Going beyond the sciences, the personal recollections of survivors themselves witness against perfectibility. A major effect of radical evil is that it sets in motion a grieving process which may not be worked through in one life span. The horror of the concentration camps or terrorist attacks is so great, the pain so nightmarish, that cyclical emotional defenses are blocked. The victimization cannot be worked through, atoned for, resolved.

The theme of incompleted grief work is the compelling thesis of Robert Lifton's research. The same motif echoes in some of the survivors' autobiographies. At the end of his memoirs Alexander Donat admits that he can neither forgive nor forget his years in the Warsaw Ghetto and several death camps.(7) Similarly, Elie Wiesel explains in a classic passage:

> Never shall I forget that nocturnal silence which deprived me, for all eternity, of the desire to live. Never shall I forget those moments which murdered my God and my soul and turned my dreams to dust. Never shall I forget these things, even if I am condemned to live as long as God himself.(8)

Do not these cries echo the sorrow of bereaved survivors, yearning to work through the tears of their grief? Is this not the purpose of telling and retelling the stories of Hitler's victims? But so long as the reign of evil is radical, then the sorrow remains a cry against a bleak and desolate universe. For in

the age of atrocity, the world is discolored with the
ashes of burned out cities. And charred human souls
lay in silence upon the earth, once vibrant with song
and laughter.

II. The Theory of Recapitulation

The work of John Hick stands as a major alternative to a distinguished group of theologies. He
classifies these as theories of recapitulation,
including the works of Paul Tillich, Karl Rahner, and
others. The latter differ from Hick by retaining the
doctrine of the Fall and by envisaging death as a
moment when life returns to its ultimate source.(9)
At the time of death evil is judged and the good
preserved forever by God. The implication is that God
remembers the good and not the evil.

Hick opposes this way of thinking, because he
doubts its realism. If--he reasons against Tillich's
theory--God only remembers the positive without the
negative, then he grants no real immortality.   God

> will not be remembering real people, because
> real people are a mixture of good and evil;
> and if everything in us less than perfect
> were   blotted   out   of   the   divine
> consciousness, there would be very little of
> us left.(10)

Hick's insight into the mixture of good and evil
is valid in terms of the biologically given tendencies
within the paroxysmal drive. But when we consider the
concrete riddle of evil and its restitution in
history, the theological problem shifts to another
level. For the issue that evil creates is not the
mixture of drives but their disintegration. It is
possible to live a normal life with the ebb and flow
of the Cain and Abel tendencies. The problem arises
when the respective needs for restitution and value
split apart, breaking down into the forms of pure evil
without the prospect of atonement.

The theological task is to find a ground for the
restitution of evil and its non-paroxysmal equivalents. In light of this criticism of Hick, we should
reconsider one of the profound intuitions in Tillich's
vision.

If we apply again the metaphor of "eternal memory," we can say that the negative is not an object of eternal memory in the sense of living retention. Neither is it forgotten, for forgetting presupposes at least a moment of remembering. The negative is not remembered at all.(11)

Tillich is not using the idea of memory in a common sense manner. It is a symbolic reference which corresponds to the notion of anamnesis. The eternal memory is a symbolically affirmed experience of acknowledging the worth of something, and separating it out from its opposite. That which is genuinely valuable is worked through and permanently preserved.

Although Tillich's description is admittedly sketchy, it conforms to the ordinary experience of grief work. Sorting out the meaning of death, working through the negative emotions, and remembering the essential worth of the deceased are all performed by bereaved survivors. This coincidence is not intentional in Tillich's theology, and it should not be understood anthropomorphically. But it does make sense as a non-causal, symbolic analogy of the divine presence.

The appropriateness of this analogy is that it further corresponds to what is central in the legacy of the survivors. Throughout their autobiographies is the appeal to memory.(12) The motive of survival is to remember the details of the experience and to be remembered. The reason for the remembrance is that the Holocaust not be repeated.

The vision of the eternal memory is necessary in order to account for an ultimate remembrance of survivors themselves and to provide for the resolution of the grief work. Since radical evil sets up a process of unfinished grief work for many, perhaps all, survivors, and since the process must be completed, then God is the only source of a transcendent resolution. It is precisely the eternal memory in God that fulfills the earthly grief work.

In the same way, the resolution of the grief also provides for a transcendent restitution. In light of radical evil, both its unlimited scope and its effects upon people, only God can draw the good out of the evil, the Abel tendency out of the Cain and the non-paroxysmal forces. Without the hope of a transcendent atonement, the struggle to bear witness in the world would have no meaning.

For these reasons, a mythic vision of a post-mortem journey of the soul is not really necessary. There is no guarantee that a pilgrimmage through ordeals in the next world would give us access to God. The only basis of consolation must come out of a divinely initiated recollection. In as much as God is transcendent and envelops the world, the divine remembrance can occur at any time and place.

In his work, John Hick does not say why a belief in life after death can resolve the problem of evil. The reason why is that the victims of radical evil usually die as mourners. If the source of evil were exclusively paroxysmal, then the victims could see a reason for their suffering and expect a movement toward restitution. But the nature of evil is not fully paroxysmal, and the possibility of atonement is not always given.

III. The Apocalyptic Ashes

The differences between John Hick and Paul Tillich illustrate a predicament that has been with us since the Protestant Reformation. In the pre-Reformation period death was understood as a climax of personal existence.(13) All life was lived in preparation for a noble death. The people hoped to achieve full contrition and serenity. For how they died was a determinate factor in their ultimate destinies. In their last hour these destinies were to be fulfilled in freedom.

The Protestant era somewhat narrowed the vision of death. John Calvin taught that the moment of death is fixed by divine decree, according to the doctrine of Predestination.(14) The end of life may be fulfilled in freedom; but the choice is God's not our own. Predestinarian belief is basically a logical inference of divine freedom. All actions are consistent with one another in the divine plan. We are not able to understand the necessity of events, because we are finite. Our task is rather to confess the glory of God in fear and reverence.

Predestinarian belief remains offensive to many, since it entails a judgment of some who are saved and some who are damned. A common criticism is that the divine decree undermines personal growth, on the one hand, and issues an unproportionate penalty, on the other. The latter point presupposes that only God is eternal and not any post-mortem domain of damnation. The finitude of all places is stipulated by the doctrine of Creation.

The most untenable aspect of Calvin's vision is the belief that God fixes the moment of death. It makes more sense to acknowledge with modern science that individual death is encoded genetically in a natural allotment. Since all cells, except cancer and sex cells, are finite and susceptible to aging, the relative span of life for each species is also limited.   Certainly, the natural span may be interrupted by fatal accidents, murder, or toxic influences.   In the absence of external factors natural death remains a personal choice.

Assigning a divine causality to the moment of death is no longer permissible on moral grounds. The sheer horror of such a limited theism grows out of the late war years in Europe. In the summer of 1944 at Auschwitz the Nazis were running low on fuel, and so the SS, to speed up the slaughter of the Hungarian Jews, chose to exterminate innocent children quickly.(15) They tossed children on top of one another, ignited them alive, all the while an orchestra played so as to conceal the screams of the dying from the near-by city. The screams of burning children reverberate as a witness against a limited theodicy.

Aside from these criticisms, there is one aspect of Calvin's vision that deserves consideration. He makes destiny an ultimate experience. Even though the primordial freedom of God is not accessible to rational inquiry, the divine relation to us is understandable through an ultimate destiny. To acknowledge a destiny of God by no means erects any limits; but it specifies that a permanent relationship with God is available beyond the natural world. That relation comes by a divine recollection.

The struggle against evil in the twentieth century has for many obliterated their freedom and wrecked their belief in God. But if we recognize that destiny is central to human experience, we have an analogical basis to understand the divine presence.

God has no one-to-one causal connection with every event in time and space. But he is present in and beyond the world in a relationship which preserves the memories of our own destinies. God does not so much decree the eternal fate of all, but he does choose to remember the good and forever exclude the evil.

Why is it necessary to affirm a transcendent destiny? One reason is that the moment of death can no longer serve as the criterion of the eternal destiny of the person. An era of mass death does not afford the opportunity for a serene and contrite last hour. It prevents the absolutizing of the final point in time.

The second reason grows out of modern science. Having exploded into being as a giant fireball, the universe is expanding ever so slowly, as the sun loses progressively four million tons of energy per second. In about eight billion years the universe will be extinguished, the vast edges collapsed, in a cataclysmic destruction. This means that human destiny unfolds in a dying universe, whose dark cavernous spaces, illumined by the brilliance of exploding stars, remain indifferent to the cries of human suffering. Our destiny mirrors a cosmic solitude.(16)

But the human task, as foreseen by Calvin, is to confess the majesty of God in fear and reverence. This confession culminates our paroxysmal natures, whether made in rage or sorrow, guilt or grief. Our confession goes beyond a simple theism and a natural theology, because it acknowledges that God alone makes restitution for the crimes of mankind. Though we come from the earth, nature is not our eternal home. Though we perish in the flames made by tyrants or in a depression caused by technology, the memory of our travail shall not pass away.

Footnotes

1. John Hick, **Death and Eternal Life** (New York: Harper, 1976), p. 157.

2. **Ibid.**, p. 418.

3. **Ibid.**, p. 309.

4. **Ibid.**, p. 209.

5. Ibid., p. 38.

6. Monod, Le Hasard et la Necessite, p. 27.

7. Donat, op. cit., n.p.

8. Elie Wiesel, Night (New York: Avon, 1969),
p. 44.

9. Karl Rahner, On the Theology of Death, trans.
by C. Henkey (New York: Herder and Herder, 1961);
Paul Tillich, Systematic Theology, III (Chicago:
University of Chicago, 1963).

10. Hick, op. cit., p. 221.

11. Tillich, op. cit., p. 400.

12. Terrence Des Pres, The Survivor (New York:
Oxford, 1976), pp. 30-33.

13. Rainer Rudolf, Ars Moriendi (Köln: Böhlau,
1957), p. 2.

14. John Calvin, Institutes of the Christian
Religion, I, trans. by H. Beveridge (Grand Rapids:
Eerdmans, 1953), p. 186.

15. Irving Greenberg, "Cloud of Smoke, Pillar of
Fire," Auschwitz: Beginning of a New Era?, ed. by E.
Fleischner (New York: KTAV, 1977), pp. 9-10.

16. Monod, op. cit., p. 186.

Index